Value
AND
Strategy

Value
AND
Strategy

COMPETING SUCCESSFULLY
IN THE NINETIES

Michael H. Shenkman

Q
QUORUM BOOKS
New York
Westport, Connecticut
London

Library of Congress Cataloging-in-Publication Data

Shenkman, Michael H.
  Value and strategy : competing successfully in the nineties / Michael H.
Shenkman.
    p. cm.
  Includes bibliographical references and index.
  ISBN 0–89930–675–6 (alk. paper)
  1. Consumer satisfaction. 2. Strategic planning. 3. Competition,
International.   I. Title.
HF5415.5.S54   1992
658.4′012—dc20   91–39712

British Library Cataloguing in Publication Data is available.

Library of Congress Catalog Card Number: 91–39712
ISBN:0–89930–675–6

First published in 1992

Quorum Books, One Madison Avenue, New York NY 10010
An imprint of Greenwood Publishing Group, Inc.

Printed in the United States of America

The paper used in this book complies with the
Permanent Paper Standard issued by the National
Information Standards Organization (Z39.48–1984).

10 9 8 7 6 5 4 3 2 1

Copyright Acknowledgments

The publisher and author are grateful to the following for granting use of
their material:

William Ouchi, *Theory Z*, © 1981, by Addison-Wesley Publishing Company,
Inc. Reprinted with permission of the publisher.

Figure 13.2 is from Gareth Morgan, *Images of Organization* (1986), p. 88.
Reprinted with permission of Sage Publishing Company.

Contents

Illustrations

Acknowledgments

This is a decidedly upbeat presentation of business life. Underlying *Value and Strategy* is the attitude that a business can be a place and can involve processes that embody constructive and affirming facets of the human endeavor. I have had the privilege of benefitting from this attitude in the course of working with scores of businesses during my career. In companies like these employees do perform up to their potential, competition is productive and fruitful, work is challenging and rewarding, and "what you contribute" is the measure of success and not "who you know" politics.

My first acknowledgment is to those visionary business people who have inspired and affirmed the optimism expressed here: Dick Winn, Tom Xhilone, Bill Tobey, and Jan Scarmuzzi most notably among them. I also acknowledge the contribution to my thoughts made by those who have suffered, unnecessarily, under conditions where this attitude is not in evidence.

Whatever value this book has is owed in large part to the love of learning instilled in the course of my liberal arts education, in general, and my studies in philosophy, in particular. To my professors and counselors, my thanks. This includes Dan Bechtel and, especially, Bo Blanchette, my mentor in philosophy and reader of the early manuscript.

I also want to thank Jeff Davis and my colleagues at Mage Centers for Management Development for seeing something worthwhile in these thoughts and for their investment in time, energy, and resources in backing its production.

My thanks to Carol Musrey for genuine companionship, inspiration of the highest order, and her loving attention to the letter and spirit of this book.

And, finally, thanks to my parents for their eternal gifts of hope and encouragement throughout my life.

Introduction: The Search for Strategy

During the last decade, one American industry after another has been rocked by international competition. In the cases of the automobile or capital equipment industries, this took the form of diminished market share; in the case of the consumer electronics industry, extinction looms. But times of crisis also present opportunities. While this sad state of affairs is unfolding, creative business decision makers and thinkers are forging a new outlook on the ways products are made and services delivered. New ideas about quality, organizational effectiveness, compensation, and recognition are being articulated and tried, with some notable success.

These ideas cluster around a central theme: A business's main job is to take care of the customer. Terms such as *total quality management*, *concurrent engineering*, and *quality circles* name some of these ideas. As we shall see, these are all pieces of a larger endeavor—to develop an approach to strategy that infuses a customer-focused commitment throughout the business's operations. The contribution of this volume is to apply a degree in philosophy and twenty years of experience in business, ten of them consulting with businesses in the United States, Europe, and Japan, to examine a wide range of business assumptions, practices, and actions through this single, customer-focused lens.

This study asks, What happens to business strategy when all of its actions are focused on customer satisfaction? The answers are dramatically different from those prescribed by some of the better known writers of what I call "classical strategies."

As we shall see, owing to their conservative and defensive nature, these strategies allow changes to overwhelm their corporate formulators. The reactions within the business community to this failure of classical strategies have been varied. Some seek out the newer models offered by other thinkers or specialized consulting firms. Others jettison any attempt at developing and utilizing a strategy altogether, seeing it as a pointless mental exercise. Both reactions to the limitations of classical strategy are shortsighted and potentially destructive.

We understand a strategy to be a viable component of business life when it provides the tools with which decision makers can contend with change. Strategy envisions, conceives, and ultimately generates change. It is precisely a strategy that is called for when business faces rapid market changes and world-class competition. But meeting these challenges successfully requires an entirely new focus, intent, and orientation for strategy, one that truly leaves the old world of business as far behind in theory as it is in fact.

CLASSICAL STRATEGIES

In response to the crisis in American business, ideas about strategy in business have both proliferated and fragmented. There are visionary strategies, competitive strategies, portfolio strategies, process strategies, "Attila the Hun" strategies, and "go with the flow" strategies. Yet, for all their differences, the strategic approaches developed during the past twenty-five years can be considered as variations on one basic definition. They all regard a strategy as an explicit pattern or framework for making decisions that, over time, combine resources and actions in an attempt to gain a competitive advantage and profits.

We call these approaches "classical" because they share certain characteristics developed during the past one hundred years of business history in the United States.

1. Classical strategies are formulated under the direction of upper management with the expectation of adoption and implementation down the line, first by lower levels of management and then ultimately by employees. They replicate military-style, top-down command structures that are designed to ensure coordinated action throughout the organization.[1]

2. They are rather elaborate statements devised to codify, if not control, the parameters of decision making and operations within the firm and to eliminate the need for decision making at the production level of operations.[2]

3. The business is placed at the center of its universe. Its products

are thought to be vehicles to generate profits, and hence return on investment (ROI) for shareholders, whereas customers are conceived as being planetary orbs, held in thrall by the force of the planners' thinking.

4. Classical strategies are essentially defensive and conservative. The planners are the defenders of home and hearth—the company's profits and ROI—as well as its hard-won markets.[3]

5. Both the company and its environment or markets are conceived as being limited in their respective abilities to absorb change.

CHANGE AND THE DECLINE OF STRATEGY

When classical strategists look at their world, they see change coming from a variety of sources. They accurately depict the intense international competition, shortened product life cycles, and rapid technical innovation that ceaselessly create downward pressures on prices and profits.

A leading proponent of one classical approach, Michael Porter contends that a business succeeds or fails to the extent that it can defend against the forces of change in its industry. In his standard-setting book *Competitive Strategy*, he names five forces that shape and define any business or industry: potential entrants, bargaining power of suppliers, bargaining power of buyers, substitute products or services, and rivalry among existing firms.[4]

Porter lists three "generic" strategies with which a company can compete in its industry: (1) *cost leadership*, in which a company adopts the lowest cost, undercutting competition or capitalizing on built-in economies of scale and experience in production, making it unprofitable for a new firm to enter; (2) *differentiation*, in which a company maintains its position by means of providing distinctive features and benefits, capitalizing on the firm's ability to uniquely serve a range or concentration of needs that no other rival would attempt; and (3) *focusing on a segment*, in which a company makes its market so specialized that others would be at a disadvantage to attempt entry. Porter goes on to say that a company must use one and only one of these strategies. He asserts that being "stuck" in the middle "is an extremely poor strategic situation."[5]

But if these strategies were equal to the conditions for which they were formulated, the companies that use them would be effective to a greater or lesser degree in fending off competition. Yet, as we see all around us, despite the acceptance of these outer-directed, market-oriented strategies, the competitive position of one American industry after another—consumer and industrial electronics, automobiles, machine tools, and other core industries—is being eroded in world-class markets. Far from being enhanced, their respective competitive positions are not even being maintained.

So we are forced to ask some questions. Will utilizing classical strategies enable a business to anticipate changes in its market or industry? Do classical strategies identify (no less comprehend) these profound changes in time to gather the planning group together, formulate a plan, disseminate and gain acceptance of the plan, and then, finally, offer products and services that constitute a meaningful response? I propose that they do not.

From the vantage point developed in this volume, we see that classical strategies deal with the downstream effects of the real causes of change. A strategy of cost leadership, for instance, responds to the fact or expectation that price cutting is inevitable. Why is this the expectation in a market? What generates price erosion? A strategy of differentiation already uses as its standard a product configuration that is established and recognized, highlighting certain aspects of that configuration to its advantage. Why is a product configured in that way? What factors successfully distinguish one feature from another? Finally, a strategy of focusing on a single market segment accepts the definitions of markets that already exist in a defined pattern as set and fixed once and for all. What factors contribute to the structure of that market in the first place?

For a strategy to be effective, it must deal with the source of the change. For us, the source of that change in the business's environment is the simple and unalterable fact that in order to meet the demands, requirements, and pleasures in their lives, people purchase the goods and services that businesses offer. This places a business and its customers in a particular and specific relationship with one another, one that we call a *value relationship*. Once established, however, those relationships do not remain static. Customers' demands, requirements, and pleasures change over time. Thus, the essential relationship a business has with its customers also must change.

THE CONCEPT OF VALUE

Value is central to our idea of strategy. It is a term we hear and use all the time, yet its meaning seems hard to pin down and put into words. Does it mean we get a good price, or a bargain, on a particular item? Is it a term that applies to anything that has a price? Does a "price" designate a specific "value" of a thing? If so, what does this value relate to—the product's usefulness, its durability, the brand nameplate it bears? Or is value something that is "completely subjective," something that is only determined individually by the one assigning the value to things on the basis of personal requirements, demands, or pleasure? If that were the case, however, how could a manufacturer assign a price to his goods? There must be some "objective" referent to the term *value*. Maybe money serves that purpose. Or does it?

Because of this confusion, the selection of the term may at first seem to be unfortunate. But with some patience, the reasons for selecting the term will become clear. To begin with, the evolution of the term *value* is instructive. Relatively speaking, *value* is a newly coined word. According to the *Oxford English Dictionary*, the term appeared in common usage during the fifteenth century as a verb, meaning "to estimate or appraise as being worth a specified sum or amount."[6] More than a century and a half later, the term was used as a noun, denoting "worth or worthiness (of persons) in respect of rank or personal qualities"; or "the relative status of a thing, or the estimate in which it is held, according to its real or supposed worth, usefulness or importance."

If one thinks back on the era during which the term arose, we can imagine that the term was "invented" (derived from the French *valoir* or the Latin *valēre*) to cope with a new world that was just emerging. New understandings about the individual, the world, and the cosmos itself were made available to more people than ever before by means of the newly invented printing press (1453). Christopher Columbus was about to make his voyage to the New World. The astronomical and mathematical groundwork was being laid by Copernicus for a revolution (in 1543) in the way the solar system would be conceived, and Kepler and Galileo were changing the way science would observe and measure nature for all time thereafter.

In the world of commerce the term took hold in the way that fore-shadows our understanding. Enterprising Europeans imported exotic goods from around the world to trade these goods for other things that were judged as having comparable worth. Since the modern monetary system was in its infancy, modified barter was still the common form of trade—a commodity such as copper, silver, or more rarely, gold was assigned a "value" in order to obtain these treasures. As time went on, the value process was extended to encompass not only luxury items but the necessities of life as well.

From this account, we can see that there are at least four ways the term has relevance for our purposes. First, our understanding of the term carries with it this sense of sellers bringing new things and services into markets to vie for customers' attention and loyalty. Second, through-out this process these new offerings change the ways people conduct their lives. Another effect of these developments on people and their society is that there is no longer a fixed or firm starting place or center that defines what the value of a thing is. Thus, third, each valued thing is capable of being itself a rubric against which other things are measured.

People contend among each other to establish the priority of things, relations, and ideas in their own lives and in the lives of those around them.

Finally, as we know it today, *value* is a term used, acted on, and lived out every day in people's lives. In fact, we have become so accustomed to the idea of value that in many ways its significance passes unnoticed. We all engage in countless valuing processes every day—from buying a newspaper to researching and shopping for a car. *Value* has come to name a set of experiences we all share as we go about making plans and provisions for our life requirements and enjoyments.

AN OUTLINE OF A STRATEGY

Certainly classical strategies are in some measure oriented to the idea of value. They all attempt to influence the buying decisions people make. In Porter's case, an aggressively low price will attract some buyers; a product that is highly differentiated, with distinctive features and benefits, will attract other buyers; and focus in a tightly defined market segment will, hopefully, yield just the right product for that segment.

But from our perspective, applying these strategies in today's world of business is like treating cancer with aspirin—attacking the most painful and visible stages of the disease, after it has advanced far along, with woefully inadequate remedies.

When we look at strategies for business, we are trying to get at the source of its problems and challenges. We are looking for the situations that lead to price cutting or that lead to the success of one feature over another. We are looking for microscopic trends that accumulate and give rise to the pressures that Porter and other classical strategists cite.

Thus, our approach has been to develop a value strategy that comprehends change in the business's core relationships so as to optimize a business's chances for success in engaging emergent challenges. In other words, it is an essential discipline that decision makers use day by day to adapt today's orientations to tomorrow's demands.

On the most general level, then, the outlook of value strategy comprises four basic elements that we shall examine in detail throughout the course of this volume:

1. A value strategy is applied within the context of a dynamic relationship between a business and its customers in order to provide people with goods and services that meet their life requirements, desires, and goals.

As we shall see, if a company's product or service is successful in meeting buyers' demands and expectations, the business will be looked to again and again to support and sustain the interactions that are made possible, necessary, and/or enjoyable by means of its product. Peter

Drucker calls this process "creating a customer," which he says is the sole reason for a business's existence.[7] We call it a process of *creating value* or creating a *value relationship* that bears with it the potential for a business's growth and profitability.

In our formulation, the value of a product or service signifies the existence—indeed, the expectation—of a specific kind of bond between the business and the buyer who uses its products or services. That bond can approach in importance the one that once existed between humans and nature alone. As people once counted on the gods to bring water, now they count on Perrier.

A flow between a business and a buyer is created, each expecting the other to behave in particular ways. The buyer expects the business to supply the product or service (in state-of-the-art form); and the business expects the buyer to purchase its products or services. When this flow, this relationship between buyer and business, is stable and fulfilled, value is "created," and a business's growth and profitability follow.

2. These relationships occur in a dynamic, changeable world market. Rather than being limited and subject to diminishing returns, this market is increasing in energy, scope, and effectiveness.

Action and change arise from any of several quarters: Consumers' tastes and requirements can change, new products and new competitors appear on the world scene, or new social or governmental mandates are imposed. Accordingly, the value relationships between a business and its customers can grow, or they can wither and die, depending on how well the business responds to customer demands, requirements, and choices.

The value relationship grows in significance and importance as a business is better able to make products available that attract, interest, and benefit people. The limitation on this growth stems more from a business's capabilities—imagination, skill, capital, will—than it does from externally determined market or competitive forces.

These forces are not acting against the company's proprietary market share but are working to change the shape, pace of change, and direction of the way people do things and the products they use to do them. These pressures set the timetable for change and point to the directions change must take. The question is not, Will the changes affect us? but rather, How and when will they affect us?

3. Businesses are composed of people, first and foremost, who are capable, willing, and even desiring to participate in productive relationships with the business's stakeholders.

Value strategy gives new meaning to the term *experience curve*. In the classical vein, this term is correlated to market share and signifies that as a company's experience with the same product grows, its costs go down. It implies that workers repetitiously deal with the same materials, machines, and procedures over and over and so can speed up their work, decreasing labor time invested in the product, thus lowering costs and increasing profits.

In value strategy, the *experience curve* refers to the capacity of everyone in the company to adapt to new conditions. The experience of working together to meet changing conditions produces structures, organizations, work patterns, and a style of capital investment that facilitate incremental change and timely response to market and customer demands.

Since no top manager will have sufficient experience to make all the necessary changes and respond to the complete spectrum of market pressures in a timely way, strategy making depends on collective inquiry into how problems can be solved and challenges met. The gap between formulation and implementation closes, and the role of upper management as the company's exclusive strategic brain trust declines. But as these shifts occur, the loss in absolute power is more than compensated because the ability of the company to undertake product innovation and organizational change increases.

4. Finally, businesses can be proactive in their markets and in their value relationships only to the extent that they give up the pretension of control and adopt the posture of creatively participating in a process that responds to the customer demands, market opportunities, and production capabilities involved in these relationships.

Our approach to strategy precludes any assumption that people will automatically buy the products a business produces. The junkyards and recycling facilities are filled with products that were never bought and so have no value. There are too many products for a buyer to choose from to assume that just any product will have value.

Our concept of value strategy begins with the question, Why does a person or business look to the market to meet this requirement in the first place, rather than find some other way? A business is not in a position to dictate anything to the consumer, but if oriented properly, it is in a position to marshal tremendous resources to meet the real requirements individual or institutional customers have with regard to its product. Rather than defending what it regards as "its share" of a market, assuming that today's market share is tomorrow's customer base, value strategy will consider each day to be one in which business people must actively participate in a relationship that transforms others into customers in the first place.

OVERVIEW

Our case is made in two parts comprising fifteen chapters. In part I, chapters 1, 2 and 3, we discuss the term *value* itself, first, as a matter of individual decision and action; second, as two specific kinds of transactions—between buyers and sellers, and then between the buyers and the products they use to participate in the activities they choose. Finally, *value* is considered as naming a special kind of relationship between a business and its customers in which value is "created." Our point in these chapters is to set down those components and nuances of the concept that make it a suitable basis on which to develop a strategy.

In chapters 4, 5, and 6, we expand our concept of value and show how markets *specify* a single product's value by placing it in the context of its availability and overall significance in people's lives and in terms of its own life span. But to this standard reading of the market, we add another dimension: that of "turnover," in which market changes are set in motion that dynamically both limit the life span of any product's value as well as point to new opportunities for innovation. This conception of how the market is formed and changed in ever shortening intervals and with ever greater impact on people's lives gives our conception of value its dynamism and expansiveness as a basis for strategy, but it also lends to our conception its sense of urgency.

This urgency stems from our understanding of the nature of competition in the new world of business. In light of our new understanding of value and markets, the notion of "competition" as it is commonly understood in classical strategies is shown to be too limited to be useful. It demands that our understanding about what competition entails in this world-class environment must be deepened and expanded.

In part II, we shift our attention to the business itself. In chapters 7 through 11, we discuss the strategic implications of the value relationship for a business's organization. We see how the business capital, organization, and energies have to be marshaled in order to meet the demands of the value relationship.

In chapters 12 through 15, we show how a value strategy reshapes the goals, structure, and managerial skills applied to the production process.

Since we are developing a new strategy for businesses, a strategy based on a deepened understanding of competitive conditions that have taken hold for real and for good only in the last twenty years, many of our terms, such as *enablement*, are new, and several familiar terms, such as *profit*, *quality*, *markets*, and *capital* are redefined. To aid the reader, we have also included a Glossary to provide ready reference to these terms.

NOTES

1. See Alfred D. Chandler, Jr., *Strategy and Structure* (Cambridge, Mass.: MIT Press, 1962).

2. Henry Mintzberg, "The Design School: Reconsidering the Basic Premises of Strategic Management," *Strategic Management Journal* 11 (1990): 171–195.

3. Michael E. Porter, *Competitive Strategy: Techniques for Analyzing Industries and Competitors* (New York: Free Press, 1980).

4. Ibid., p. 4.

5. Ibid., p. 41.

6. J. A. Simpson and S.S.C. Weiner, preparers, *Oxford English Dictionary*, vol. 12 (Oxford: Clarendon Press, 1989), pp. 415–418.

7. Peter Drucker, *Management: Tasks, Responsibilities, Pactices* (New York: Harper & Row), p. 61.

Part I

The Value Process

1

Value as Experience and Decision

We divide our discussion of the value concept into three chapters. Chapter 1 considers value to be a special kind of personal experience and decision-making process. For a consumer, the buying process is neither strictly rational nor merely compulsive. It is a process that feeds into and connects with other facets and dimensions of people's lives, and it does so over an extended period of time.

Chapter 2 considers *value* as a term that encompasses specific kinds of dealings or transactions between people, between people and the products they buy, and between people and businesses. Every individual determines a product's value in terms of a solitary experience with it, but he or she obtains that product and uses it only by means of exchange. Most economic accounts of value focus on this aspect of value.

But we have to take into account that value is an outcome of a process in which a user is not primarily focused on the product in question. Users are ultimately concerned with how that product performs in the activities in their daily lives—how well it serves as a means to accomplish goals and tasks. Just as important, if users want to continue to use the product in their daily lives—if they want to drive cars, use computers, drink bottled water—they must be assured that the product will be supported or enhanced in the future.

Finally, in chapter 3, we take a closer look at the relationship between the customer and the business that provides the product to see how value is created. We will see that value is created only if a buyer feels confident that the investment required in time, energy, and money to incorporate the product into his life will be sustained in the future by being able to continue this activity. This value relationship has to be the focus and driving force of all strategy.

Our focus in this chapter is value as the experience of a buyer, which is the basic and fundamental level of value. A product's or service's value is established only when a person moves through a complete set of three specific experiences: prospection, projection, and procurement. In *prospection*, a person resolves to change a situation by means of purchasing a product or service. *Projection* summarizes the actions in which a person concretely imagines and rehearses the new interactions the prospective product or service will entail. In *procurement*, a person first matches the projection to those products that are available and within reach, then buys the item, and finally engages in the activities it facilitates.

PROSPECTION

The value process begins when a person experiences the desire to interact with other people or with things in order to resolve a deficit or lack. Social psychologists refer to this condition or psychological state as being one of stimulation or arousal or having some incentive. They point to a combined physiological and psychological state in which dissatisfaction with a bodily or environmental condition induces action. Hunger, thirst, and feeling emotional discomfort or anxiety are typically referred to as *deficit conditions*. But to these immediate, physiological stimulations we would also add the experienced socially oriented lacks such as not having a car or a computer or a washing machine—lacks that pertain to current social or cultural standards for accomplishing one's daily tasks.

There are other characteristics to the desire-inspired incentive that motivate action. Since a specific situation or lack is being addressed in order to bring about another situation, there is also a specific *intention* involved; and specific means will be applied to resolve the situation. Desire that initiates a valuing process must lead to motivated and attentive action that changes things or conditions for that person. For instance, I can have a secret, passionate yearning for the love of a woman. Or, I can have a wish to be a singer. But unless these wishes and hopes become a defining, crystallizing element of my actions and decisions, they are not what we mean by *value-producing desire*.

At the stage of prospection, when I am stimulated to act, I do not necessarily have a definite solution in mind. At this moment, I am absorbed in the prospect of changing the present situation and envisioning a future situation that will be better—or at least will maintain a desirable status quo. What is known is that action is necessary. A process of assessment has begun that will sort, select, and guide products that make those actions possible.

Commitment

Regardless of the level of refinement of the person's resolve at this point in the process, a person is potentially initiated into a value process when he or she makes a commitment to a course of action that will bring about a change regarded as desirable and/or necessary. Commitment, as we understand it, orients a person toward the future—changing circumstances or maintaining one that is desired—in such a way that guides actions on the basis of the contribution those actions make toward that ultimate intention. In pursuit of a lover, he will go to places he knows the object of his love will also be in attendance; to pursue a singing career, she will sing often and strengthen her voice.

Since our focus is on how a value relationship develops between buyers and businesses, we add to this generalized view that the intentions, commitment, and actions that lead to a value relationship are channeled toward the goods and services businesses provide. Most aspects of the lover's desire and commitment to action will never enter a value process because the object and means of attaining it are not produced by business. But when he buys flowers, jewelry, or other gifts to lure and entice his amorous object, a value process does come into play. An erstwhile singer will become involved in a value process only if she sets out to retain the services of a professional singing coach, whose business is to offer that service.

Envisioning

In terms of the value process we are describing here, the significant action that occurs in prospection is that when a situation must be affected and changed, the future is envisioned. The committed person puts several components together: identifying the specific lack, envisioning the desired remedy, and also envisioning the means by which the new situation will be achieved. Value thus signifies an intention that is fully conscious and, to a greater or lesser degree, thought out in advance.

We can assume that the solution envisioned will not worsen the original state but will aim in a positive, affirming direction, aiming to optimize a situation or expand the options available. The intention is to establish the best situation, one that affords the most possibilities and/or chances for fulfilling the commitment, by connecting a limited and specific intention to a wider spectrum of ideas, associations, products, and services. The singer's choice of a coach will be made on the basis of this coach's stature in the music world, for instance, as well as on the basis of the coach's talent or cost.

PROJECTION

Projections consist of the conscious thoughts about the lacking or deficient situation and the possibilities that can change it or maintain it. In the value process, these thoughts are directed toward specific products and services that are known to be generally available and are sufficient means by which to address the situation. But while these thoughts are oriented outward, both at products and toward the future, there are inner-directed thoughts as well. These thoughts are immersed in the person's psychological conditioning and real-life circumstances.

Conditions and Circumstances

In the projection step, a person considers an array of products and services. There will be choices between similar products and/or services that take the same approach to a situation, and there will also be choices that offer entirely different approaches to the situation. But this projection is not completely freewheeling or free-form. The projection always occurs within limiting conditions and circumstances. While the person projects in detail what means—tools, instruments, interactions— can be applied to the situation, this process will also include inner-directed considerations.

- The person is always situated within specific circumstances of geography and the region's economic development, personal income, education, and information channels that filter out solutions, rendering them inaccessible or unknown.

- The person is similarly conditioned by thoughts on how the experience with the product will proceed. There are more or less rational considerations, such as how the product will affect circumstances, whether it will engender unexpected results or unanticipated costs, and how the outcome will be maintained and what that maintenance will cost. But on the less rational side, the feelings, images, and emotions that the new activity will engender are also considered. Issues such as security, familiarity, self-confidence in one's adaptability and talent, how life will change, and how it will feel using such things—all subjective intangibles—are projected onto the process.

- The projected solution is also influenced by attitudes, norms, and beliefs. Amish beliefs proscribe buying automobiles or zippers, so their solutions will not involve most commercially available products. If a person develops a bad attitude toward a product, owing to a bad sales pitch or a defective product, the projected solutions will often attempt to skirt these products. When the awareness of environmental issues took hold, projected solutions also had to take into account pollution and protecting natural resources. Beliefs, attitudes, and norms are all components of one's predisposition toward the actions one will take to resolve a commitment.

Elimination

Projection is a process that formulates the actions and products that will fulfill the commitment by placing more and more real-life considerations into the picture. When this is considered in the context of the value process, projection leads to an elimination process, a scaling down of the options available to those that fit with the person's realistic self-appraisal.

Options that are too expensive or inconsistent with one's values are eliminated, and options that are affordable and consistent with one's real life are selected for further consideration. Some writers render this elimination process in the form of a hierarchical decision tree.[1] Each branch has many smaller branches from which a selection is made before moving on to the next branching selection.

Different constituents of a person's conditioning factors are called to the fore at each juncture.[2] When a buyer confronts an array of product choices—those in the same category and those in competing categories—the selection and/or valuing process does not occur on the proverbial "level playing field." The field is contorted by the buyer's orientations, beliefs, habits, and the like, as well as by the range of knowledge about the product or service.[3] Only if there are products that get through this highly complex, individualistic, and idiosyncratic filter will the decision process continue to the next step.

PROCUREMENT

While the previous two phases can go on more or less in the privacy of one's mind, procurement is a fully *interactive* step. Procurement begins when a prospective buyer sets out to acquire a product or service that has been projected to be a means to resolve the situation and fulfill the commitment. Interactions include all the activities it takes to make the acquisition: telephone calls; visits to stores, shops, and showrooms; talks with salespeople and service people. This and subsequent steps in the process involve information gathering, negotiating or bargaining between people, and agreeing on or signing contracts of exchange.

Context

As we saw in the projection step, a buying decision is always made in the context of choices and comparison, judgment, and evaluation. The projection process detailed the specifics of the intention in light of what choices were available and what resources a prospective buyer can allocate to the product, and so on. The procurement process resolves the issue of what specific means will adequately fulfill the conclusions arrived at in the projection. The product or service is thus finally judged on the merits of its specific features and benefits (differentiation) and (comparative) price. These components of the judgment are then matched to personal considerations enumerated during the projection phase of the process.

Extension

The value process extends beyond the act of buying and even beyond the life span of the particular product. After the purchase has been made, as the product is being used, all the emotional, attitudinal, and affective factors that led to the decision are retraced in the form of evaluation and reconsideration of the product. What was promised is assessed against the reality of using the product.

That is, the promises of ease, comfort, and security using a new model food processor, for instance, will be tested against actual results. It is not just the features and benefits of the appliance that will be tested and evaluated. The complete experience of preparing foods is assessed against the expectations erstwhile gourmets had when they bought the product. The ease and speed of the slicing/dicing operation versus the time required to clean the processor in between uses, as well as the results obtained—beautifully julienned carrots—are all taken into consideration.

But the immediate encounter does not end the evaluation. The product or service will be evaluated, judged, and assessed long after the hands-on encounter with it has expired. The experience of the activity will reinforce the buyer's original expectations, will be on a par with the buyer's expectations, or will pale in comparison to what was originally envisioned. The experience will be judged to be fitting or in conflict with the person's specifying projections.

Most likely to be judged positively is the product that is indispensable to the particular activity involved. The more the product makes the activity possible to begin with (such as a computer makes word processing possible), the more the value of that product stands out as compelling and defining.

From this extended consideration of the product's value, we can see that this process does not necessarily lead to a repetition of the same purchase the next time around. It is just as likely that the initial experience leads to the purchase of another product that builds on the capabilities opened by the original product but not provided for by the original. The purchase of a low-power or dedicated word processor, for instance, is likely to lead to the purchase of a more powerful and more versatile computer. The value process engenders the desire to continue in an activity. As it does, and people become accustomed to the activity and its products, they expect improvements and enhancements. Thus, the value process also promotes changes to the products it supports.

Summary of Value Process Experience

Stage in the Valuing Process	Buyer's Experience	Value Action
Prospection	Commitment	Envisioning
Projection	Conditions and circumstances	Elimination
Procurement	Context	Extension

QUALITY AND THE CIRCLE OF VALUE

Up until now, the buyer has undergone a valuing process in which the decision to apply a particular product or service to a situation is either validated or invalidated, supported or abandoned (see the table above). But there must be more to the experience if value is to be created. Value is only created when the evaluation of the product is complete throughout the course of its use *and* the buyer intends to use the product again to maintain or enhance the situation it addresses.

So the full cycle that is required to establish the value of a product or service actually entails going through the sequence of prospection, projection, and procurement at least twice. During the first half cycle, the process is rather speculative and tentative, experimental at best. Each step along the way is done warily, with circumspection and criticism.

The second half of the cycle repeats the "P-P-P" steps, but its intent is quite different from the first time around. In this second cycle, the product is familiar; all features and benefits of the product are known, specific, and concrete. The buyer is then in the position to ask, Is this the product that best enables me to meet my requirements?

Another crucial assessment that is going on in the second phase of the cycle is a judgment that goes beyond the product itself. Here the buyer is asking whether or not the provider of the product or service involved will be in business in the long run. The question is not only, Is the business surviving? but also, Is this business committed to this activity itself, to making this activity a positive, constructive, and enhancing experience? This question is important for the simple reason that if a person is making a commitment to doing something new, he or she wants to be assured that the investment in time, energy, and money will pay off.

In the early eighties, for instance, many people bought IBM personal computers (PCs). The reason many chose IBM over the products of the company that invented the PC, Apple, was their confidence in the belief that IBM would be around to answer questions and provide product enhancements down the road. No one could, at that point, have such confidence in the fledgling company, founded by countercultural geniuses in a Silicon Valley garage.

The issue in this instance, and in any value relationship, is whether the experience of both the activity and the product or service that supports it is sufficiently affirming to establish a continuing relationship between the buyer and the business that provides the product. When the experience is sufficiently affirming and/or is deemed necessary, the product or service has become an established and accustomed part of the way people accomplish goals and resolve situations in life. The value of the product or service signifies two things: First, it is useful in enabling people to engage in activities in a way that accords with social standards and practices; and second, the product or service fits into the pattern of things, meanings, and associations that make life worthwhile and fulfilling.

This aspect of value is what is generally understood as quality. *Quality* is a term that is applied to those experiential characteristics of the product or service that come to the attention of the buyer in its role of meeting life requirements. The quality of the product is that component of its value that helps to define the experience of the activity, either positively, neutrally, or negatively.

The product's features and benefits are surely noted. But quality goes beyond bells and whistles, to how the new activity the product makes possible fits into the style, texture, and vitality of the buyer's life. *Quality* summarizes the judgment of whether the product used in the activity meets, falls short of, or exceeds the standards that were originally envisioned.

How much a person will pay, how often a person will reinvest in a product, and what specific configuration of features and level of quality will all depend on how well the product integrates into that person's life activities, plans, and goals. Only quality leads to value because only a product that can actively shape the decision as to how a buyer will resolve his requirements will be chosen the next time out.

Thus, to the person involved in a buying decision, there is nothing abstract about the value of the product or service. My PC is so integral to the way I do my work that it has become "invaluable." Its value signifies that I do many things—from writing documents to balancing my checkbook—in ways that are only possible by means of a PC. My experience of writing and doing calculations is shaped by the PC, and my expectations of how these operations will proceed, the time they will take, and the formats they will appear in are all based on using my computer.

In this way, a product is valued because it has become a fixture and extension of that life-style and takes its place in the person's hierarchy of requirements and methods for attaining satisfaction in life. A product that is not valued—my food processor, for instance—sits on a shelf for a time and then disappears from the store shelves as well, a nonentity, neither noticed nor missed.

NOTES

1. Amos Tversky and Shmuel Sattath, "Preference Trees," in *Choice Models for Buyer Behavior*, McAlister Leigh, ed. (Greenwich, Conn.: JAI Press, 1982), pp. 201–232.

2. Lawrence A. Crosby and Darrel D. Muehling, "External Variables on the Fishbein Model: Mediation, Moderation or Direct Effects?" *Advances in Consumer Research* 10 (1982): 95; and Wayne D. Hoyer, "Variations in Choice Strategies Across Decision Contexts: An Examination of Contingent Factors," *Advances in Consumer Research* 13 (1985): 32–36.

3. Hoyer, "Variations in Choice Strategy"; and Mihaly Csikszentmihalyi and E. Rochberg-Halton, *The Meaning of Things: Domestic Symbols and the Self* (New York: Cambridge University Press, 1981), pp. 186–187.

2

Value in Action: The Transaction

So far we have talked about how value develops during the course of buyers' concrete and lived experiences with the products and services they use in daily life. We showed how value is created only when the product can be counted on over the long term to maintain or enhance buyers' life-styles.

But we all know the value process is not one that is completed by one person in isolation. It is a *social* process. Creating value involves at least two people but usually scores of people who conduct themselves in a prescribed manner. Therefore, implicit throughout the buyer's experience were two types of transactions. The first type is the *deal*, in which a buyer, beginning the procurement steps, meets those sellers who offer products that attempt to meet his requirements. The second type is the *enablement* transaction, in which the product or service is used.

THE DEAL

We now introduce a new player into the value process. As we know, before a buyer can make a deal, he or she has to meet the seller. By definition, if a buyer and seller do not meet, and if they do not come to an agreement that puts a new capability in the buyer's hands, and something of equated value in the seller's hands, value cannot be created. The seller sets the entire value process within the context of a relationship that encompasses both the buyer's anticipations, meanings, and requirements as well as the business's intentions and requirements.

Upon entering the value process, both the buyer and seller make something available to someone else, and both want something other than what they now have. The buyer has something he is willing to apply toward the procurement of something else, usually money, and wants a product or service that will meet requirements for resolving a situation. When a buyer has money to spend, he has choices and options and options for what value relation he will enter and how that relationship will evolve. Of course, he does not have to spend any of that money. It can be deposited in a bank or hidden under a mattress. Because the buyer has money, he can have confidence that the value process will provide a more or less satisfactory outcome.

The seller, on the other hand, owns a specific thing (or service) that will yield the results she wants only if a buyer is found for it. She owns her item strictly for the purpose of selling it. To the extent that the seller still possesses her commodities, she owns nothing but anxiety. Her resources have been speculatively concentrated into a single commodity, which is exchangeable only in the specific circumstances for which it was designed and suits specific buyers, who must be found. The seller's confidence, such as it is, is based on the adequacy of her forecasts and market knowledge but not on any definite knowledge about how the future will unfold.

So the buyer may be more or less dependent on the value process, depending on the priority the intended purchase has in his life. But the seller will survive only if a buyer wants to own the specific commodity she offers.

Thus, the value process begins in a condition of doubled desire: two people seeking each other out in order to resolve each of their distinct and compelling situations. The buyer must contend with a variety of seller strategies. A seller, on the other hand, not only must meet the requirements of the buyers but must project and establish how her products or services distinctively and singularly satisfy the buyer's demands.

The first type of value transaction we consider, the deal, has four steps. The first of these actually gets under way when the buyer enters the procurement step of the valuing process and goes *shopping*. By this act, he enters an entire system that is established solely to support the deal-making transactions: to facilitate the process of giving buyers ready access to sellers' wares and making exchange both easy and, as far as possible, pleasant. Stores, shopping plazas and malls, highways, and parking lots are key components of this system. In many industries, the seller brings this procurement system to the buyer and takes on direct responsibility for all the tasks required for making a sale. In this case, the buyer elicits the attention of more than one seller in order to generate a choice between competing options.

Sellers have erected and maintained this system and specialize in emphasizing considerations that will appeal to potential buyers. The retail industry contributes order, targeting, and segmentation to the process, enabling sellers to maximize the access and availability of goods to prospective buyers, putting the right products conveniently where those people most likely to buy them will go. The system is also organized to present information that will help to move the product into buyers' hands.

The seller's job is to create the kind of movement that will advance and even energize the valuing process in her direction. One intention of the system is to influence buyers' decisions—solidify or correct them in light of realities. Another intention is to shift the balance of power in the seller's favor, to whatever extent possible, by transforming the buyer's commitment into an attraction and/or decision about a specific product.

Once this is done, the deal moves to the next step, that of *appraisal*. During this step, buyers survey all the choices that approach the criteria for resolving their requirements. Buyers make an attempt to see all the product variations, features, and benefits different sellers present; to understand how and why they are packaged together into various configurations; and to determine at what price they are available. These packages will then be measured against their projections. Maybe they can get more for their money than they originally thought; maybe one person's benefit is just an added expense to another. Given the array of products to choose from, however, a buyer can often put a custom package together and match those features against very specific and personal requirements.

Meanwhile, the seller is performing an appraisal of her own. Her first job in this phase is to ferret out the salient factors that are driving the decision of the single (or aggregate) buyer. She also "qualifies" the buyer in terms of income, demographics, life-style, and the like, to determine if this is a likely prospect. She also finds out what steps will be necessary to complete the deal. Will a married couple have to decide jointly, or is one person in charge? If dealing with a company, who are the actual decision makers? What does the company buyer's evaluation and purchasing process entail?

Once the buyer has assimilated all the factors of the appraisal, matched them to the pertinent requirements, he may choose to open a *negotiation*, the third step in the deal. In this phase of the process, the crucial interactions take place that set the tone and parameters of evaluation that affect the remainder of the buyer's experience with the product or service.

While it is true that a negotiation has to do with setting a price— getting the price down, for the buyer; maximizing it, for the seller— this is only part of the story. The negotiation has several crucial components that fall outside this specific objective. For instance, negotiations began with promotions and advertising that positioned the product and created an image, a set of expectations, that the buyer carries with him into the stores and showrooms. In this sense, the negotiation began long before the buyer and seller met.

But more important for us, the negotiation is the first moment when the value process becomes an actual relationship. At this point the buyer is opening up to the possibility of meeting the seller's price. The negotiation also determines the criteria the buyer will apply in order to gauge how successful the product is during the course of its use. Most important, however, is the fact that the negotiation begins to shape both parties' subsequent behavior toward each other.

The seller will emphasize certain features and benefits that will constitute near-contractual promises (in some kinds of negotiations, they are contractually cemented) before the sale is made. These promises set conditions that may endure long after the sale. The buyer will make specific decisions that confirm or reshape his projections, based on the descriptions, terms, and promises made by the seller in the course of the negotiation.

Many of these factors will be reflected in the price that is agreed on in advance of the final step in the deal, the *exchange*. At this point, the transaction has moved to the level of there being an actual agreement between the parties. Each gives up something that has significance, although the significance of the items is quite different for each party; and each gains something else that each wants.

The exchange creates a moment in which events are, to a greater or lesser degree, irreversible. Prior to this moment, each party can walk away, with nothing but time and some money, invested and maybe some feelings hurt or validated. Once the exchange takes place, however, the value process is locked in place with parameters, agreements, and expectations that have a price attached to each, as determined by the negotiation. This by no means consummates the value relationship we are seeking. But, at the very least, now firmly in place are all the elements and parameters that will either make or break the process as it moves toward such a relationship.

ENABLEMENT

If we were looking at the process of valuing commodities "economically," or were attempting to trace the process by which wealth and profits are generated, the deal, culminating in the exchange, would comprise all the moments in which value was assessed and acted on. The buyer would have a commodity, and the seller would have a cache of money (and would have made a bit of profit along the way). One can view such exchanges in the aggregate and surmise from there how a social economy progresses, defines itself, and grows.

But for us, all that has happened so far is that the business's past investments have produced a modest return. While an economist can be satisfied with a presentation of value that shows that there are returns from production, a value strategy must go deeper into the process and comprehend what elements of the process yield returns for it, specifically, amid all the products that are available.

To reach this level of understanding, we shift our attention to a new phase of the transaction wherein the product becomes an enablement for the buyer. In this type of transaction, the buyer interacts in his own world in a way that is only possible and achieves outcomes that are only possible by means of this product or service. The activity represents a new capability for the buyer. It is in this role as *enabling* a user to undertake a new interaction, one that is specific to the features and characteristics of the business's product, that the transaction actually fulfills the conditions and promises of the value process.

Enablement Versus Need

This aspect of our concept, that a person is undertaking a new interaction or seeking to establish a new situation, is what distinguishes our concept of the value process from a related concept—that of need.

We understand a *need* to be an immediately experienced, limited, and definite feeling a person has that leads to a compulsion to take action, to remedy an environmental or bodily lack or deficiency. Once that psychological condition is sated, the need disappears. At stake for the needy person is not any particular remedy but any remedy that satisfies the need and quiets the compulsion. But then the need arises again and again, and is satisfied again and again, in virtually the same form, by the same agent or material.

So for us the difference between a thing that satisfies a need and an enabling product (enablement) or service that has the potential to be valued, or to create value, is this: Goods or services that satisfy needs are applied to conditions, impulses, and drives that people do not or cannot control, whereas an enablement is applied to those aspects of life—orientations and conditions—a person has decided to affect or control.

When engaged in a valuing process, people are resolving situations that include merely satisfying immediate physical, psychological, or environmental needs. But at the same time, these people, when engaged in the valuing process involving products and services businesses offer, consider factors that encompass a much wider range of life-style choices and options. People involved in value decisions seek out a resolution that will not so much satisfy the immediate lack as it will enable them to act and engage and interact with the world in a way that they envision and choose.

For example, when I get thirsty, I have no choice about physiological thirst or the need to drink a liquid. That need will arise again and again, repetitiously, in the same form. And I can, if I so choose, satisfy it or quench the thirst, again and again, in the same manner with a drink of water. Once sated, the need will, in fact, disappear for a time. There does not have to be any valuing process involved in the drive to quench my thirst, especially if I live near a freshwater source.

In contrast to this, however, the value process expands consideration of the means for resolving the immediate desire beyond the immediate impulse. It points to a resolution that has longevity or continuity over time, and further, one that is integrated with other products and activities that have significance in my life.

In the context of a value process, I am not *just* thirsty. I am thirsty, to be sure, but what I *want* is a beer. I am aiming to resolve a situation that has many nuances, one component of which is thirst. When I get the beer and drink it down, the thirst is quenched, but the valued components remain active. These include considerations of taste, texture, and feel of the product (as made consistently available in a particular product) as it goes down and possibly the setting and associations I have with this particular beverage (a favorite pub, good times, slight "buzz" from the alcohol).

Of course, the way this experience that links thirst with the commodity of beer enters one's mind is, "I am thirsty for a beer; I *need* a beer." The value component becomes *identified* with the biological impulse. When I experience thirst, I immediately think, "Beer." This is just what beer producers hope will happen, of course.

If, continuing along this line, I go one step further, beyond merely thinking, "Beer," and think of a specific *kind* of beer, such as Sam Adams, then I have made the leap that establishes a "brand." The brand specifically represents the wider and more encompassing associations that extend beyond the immediate impulse or need. These are the associations that for me indicate value and signify that I will have a multifaceted, satisfying experience in the process of quenching my thirst.

Steps of the Enablement Transaction

As we understand it, then, the enablement type of transaction has three steps: appropriation, incorporation and use, and reconsideration.

In the *appropriation* step, a buyer takes the product home (or begins interacting with the service provider); opens the box; and engages in thoughts, assessments, and actions that will foster its use in the buyer's specific setting and situation. At this point, the product must directly address the situation originally envisioned, and it must accord with the expectations laid out during the buyer's prospection and projection. Then, the product must be intelligible, so that the buyer can quickly establish a rapport or level of comfort, and the activity can begin.

Incorporation and use comprises all actions the buyer undertakes with the product in hand, so to speak. *Incorporation* takes into account the time it takes for the product-enabled activity not only to be learned but to be internalized, habituated, and adopted as one's own. And then the product is used more or less automatically as an adjunct to the activity the product enables.

In the course of the incorporation and use phase, the product may be used up, leading to the final step of the enablement transaction: the *reconsideration* step. This is the critical step at the end of the product's useful life where the buyer decides whether or not to continue in the activity the product enables. If the decision is to continue participating in the activity, the buyer asks, What product or service should I use in the future? The answer to this question determines whether or not a product offered by a business will have value.

Enablement and Value

People have entered into the enablement transaction because, and only because, they envision that a certain activity will take place that will resolve a specific situation for the better. No matter what bells and whistles a product or service may have, if it does not advance a task at hand, a task that I at some level want or choose to engage in, it will be judged as having little or no value.

A product or service in the incorporation and use stage of the enablement transaction is judged to have value when, at a minimum, it does advance the envisioned task and resolves the situation at hand. But it becomes prized—held in some esteem, talked about favorably or enthusiastically—when it enhances the experience of participating in an activity that I choose, such as using my PC for producing documents, or driving a quiet, tight-handling, and peppy car. In the final step, reconsideration, these factors are assessed. In this step, the buyer first reflects on the status and meaning the activity has in life; the reconsideration only later moves to reflect on the product's or service's specific characteristics.

Value, Utility, and Profit

Having reached this point, let us ask, What has this process accomplished? In general, it has set in motion a series of very specific transactions between people that would not have occurred if not for the existence of the product or service and the corresponding buyer's desire to use it. In the course of these transactions a new operating context, a new means for conducting specific activities with other people and between people and products, is established. Change has been generated and freely adopted by a wide spectrum of participants.

For us, this means that the value of the product is not dependent on its utility but rather on the extent to which that utility is perceived as resolving and/or enhancing significant situations for people in appropriate and meaningful ways. Only in a static, unchanging market will value appear to be related to a thing's utility. In that kind of situation, a thing's utility is mistaken for its value because people use the same products over and over again. It appears that the product's value resides in its utility because, at this time, it is the only product that performs these tasks or makes an activity possible.

In other words, if only one version of a hammer were available to drive in nails, I would equate the value of the hammer with its useful capacity (its utility), to drive in nails, because that is the only way I could drive in nails (other than using the nearest rock). But all that changes once competing hammers come on the scene—hammers of different sizes, some with rubber-covered grips, others with wooden handles. Once this happens, it becomes clear that the value any hammer has will be determined by how well it supports my experience of driving in nails.

The point is that as soon as people have many products to choose from and as soon as businesses make available to people a wide range of activities in which to use many different kinds of products and services, the thing's value does not depend only on its utility, but instead becomes dependent on the choices people make in their lives about which products they will use and also which products best compliment their expectations and demands.

In the context of value, this gives a new significance to the selling process as well. Selling is not a simple matter of pushing product out the door or "delivering the goods." Selling creates whole contexts in which prospective options for expanding one's capabilities can be envisioned by potential buyers. It acts as a progenitor of value by energizing the process of change, by creating, even by anticipating the milieu of style or meaning that makes products viable, which in turn creates demand. The new context opened up by the enablement must be proved, validated to the buyer. It must be enhanced and integrated through supporting exchanges to the extent that the product is shown to have sufficiently broad and/or central application to warrant a buyer's expenditure.

Change and selling exist in a symbiotic relationship to one another. Change can happen because selling paves the way. A seller helps buyers to get comfortable with new ideas and new forms of interaction. Selling may be considered to be a methodology by which a business can confidently present new options and integrate them into a comprehensive picture for a buyer. The process of selling is an exercise in making commodities "desirable, yet reachable."[1]

This is a process in which, at least potentially, both the buyer and the business gain. The gain for the buyer is in being able to participate in a new set of life-enhancing activities that the product enables or makes possible. The gain for the business is its profit. In our understanding, profit is never about technological advancements or flashy product features. Profits follow when a business establishes a relationship in which people look to it as being a vital provider of important products that serve as enablements in their daily lives.

Peter Drucker calls this essential role of a business "creating a customer," creating a relationship in which a person is accustomed to using this product in the course of everyday activities at work and at home. When a business fosters and consolidates this kind of a relationship, it converts a value-based transaction into a value relationship.

NOTE

1. Arjun Appadurai, "Introduction: Commodities and the Politics of Value," in *The Social Life of Things: Commodities in Cultural Perspective* (New York: Cambridge University Press, 1986), p. 55.

3

Strategy and Creating Value

FROM THE VALUE PROCESS TO THE VALUE RELATIONSHIP

So far we have seen that the value concept is applied to situations in which someone purchases and uses an enablement—a means, tool, or instrument, in the form of a particular product, that enables that person to do a certain activity in a specific way—to optimize or resolve a situation in everyday life, at work or at home. If the product serves its purpose well, it will assume an important role in the person's life. The business that supplies that product has the opportunity to sustain a relationship when the buyer seeks to continue with that activity by purchasing the enabling product again.

When people in a business take up that opportunity, they commit themselves to several kinds of actions: to make products and offer services that contribute to people's lives; to ensure ready access to them; to provide the facilitating information and mechanisms that permit easy incorporation into people's lives; and to provide assurance of continued support of the product and development of its enabling properties in the future.

In this way, the value process shapes the lives of everybody involved—the customers' lives as well as the lives of the members of the business organization—to the actions required to sustain and even promote the use of this particular enabling product. When this cycle becomes "normalized" and anticipated by all parties involved, the value process we have described so far converts into the value relationship.

When some people mold their actions to provide a product and others mold theirs to use that product, it becomes what we might call *a cultural artifact*—an accepted medium of relation, exchange, decision, and interaction. Value is created because new conditions and opportunities for interacting between people based on this product are developed and sustained. Because of this product, new ways of doing things are opened up, and new institutions or businesses are created. These product-enabled activities become valued to the extent that they expand the horizons—contribute to specific life-style behaviors—of individuals who willingly devote their resources to them.

So when a person decides to buy a product once again, the value process is no longer undertaken abstractly or conceptually, in isolation. At that point, a new dimension of the transactions we described earlier opens up. The series of transactions becomes a *relationship* in which there is mutual recognition and reciprocity between a buyer and a business. The experience with the product is now a shared enterprise. We say that value is created because a new set of relationships and new activities are created, not just for one buyer but for several people, that are based on the interactions the business's enabling products and services make possible.

The money and goods that change hands in the exchange represent a "currency" in the sense of creating a self-reinforcing flow of production and subsequent use, which in turn creates the need for more production, and so on. As the currency flow stabilizes and becomes more or less (never absolutely) anticipated by both parties, the relationship takes on the character of being an objective, substantial fact of life—something both parties count on as being integral and accepted aspects of their lives.

For the business, the buyers' return to its product constitutes recognition for its efforts. Profitability, in this light, measures the product's priority or status in people's lives. If the business is to survive, decision makers know they must meet the expectations of buyers. They must consistently provide the same level of quality and satisfaction in subsequent transactions that they established at first. Sales and profits betoken the fact that buyers have embraced the new way of doing things and the enablement has been accepted and even anticipated. They signify that a value relationship has in fact been firmly established.

The value relationship between buyers and a business completes a circuit. Buyers elect to engage in a particular set of activities that entails the use of a specific product. They value this way of doing things and thus form connections, associations, and commitments (of time, money, and personal energy) associated with this activity. The business, on the other hand, makes the product available so that the interaction may take place and ensures that the relationship, once established, can be continued and/or enhanced in subsequent product life cycles.

Creating value only occurs when people orient their activities, decisions, and modes of conduct around the fact of, and in expectation of, there being specific products and services available. To ensure availability, businesses dedicate the thought, energy, and material resources that are necessary.

The premise of value strategy is that people in the business fully devote themselves to the positive and constructive role of providing products that enable people to engage in specific activities in their daily lives. To the extent that it does (or must) provide opportunities for new activities, business is a powerful force for change in individual lives and for the society as a whole. When these activities enhance the quality of life for people, business participates in a constructive process, and its profits measure social health and well-being.

VALUE AND STRATEGY

When we think of creating value in these terms, we can see that a strategy comprises the concepts, decisions, and actions that are necessary to establish, sustain, and enhance a more or less necessary relationship between a business and its customers. This also directs our thinking about strategy in new directions. In general, these new directions have four fundamental components that underpin all that follows in subsequent chapters:

1. Value strategy is directed at conceiving, making, and selling products that contribute to the quality of people's daily lives, at work and at home. Strategy defines and specifies consumer activities that give rise to enablements that people require in their daily lives.

Value strategy focuses on

- designing and building a product or service that will sustain high performance throughout the entire course of its use;
- communicating information about the product or service in a way that fits and enhances people's understanding of its possibilities as an enablement;
- establishing networks and mechanisms that ensure continued availability; and
- providing products and services that take into account the full dimensions of the prospects and projections that people currently use to frame a buying decision, including how people want to enhance their life activities by means of this enablement.

This does not mean merely creating products "with all the bells and whistles" or adding on "distinctive" features and benefits to existing products or services. From the perspective of value strategy, no need is satisfied in isolation, no product is merely consumed and disappears. When the product or service is immersed in the value process, its features and benefits, on their own merit, may not constitute the determining issue in any particular buying decision. No product itself has "intrinsic value."

Even a piece of fruit, a banana, is immersed in a host of connecting and competing associations. A banana satisfies hunger, but the bunch of bananas or the oranges you buy are marked with a company name or logo. This branding is supposed to signify value-related indications of quality, a sense of assurance that in terms of the experience of satisfying the need (not merely meeting it with something or other) this is the best product available.

Strategically, this translates into the realization that making a good product is only part of the battle—and not necessarily its most important aspect. It is just as important to produce the *right* product—that is also a good product—that is available and well integrated into the stream and flow of people's lives. This kind of consideration is neither a technical matter nor a matter of competitive marketing. It is a matter of fully appreciating the quality of the experience that the product enables.

A strategy must carefully take into account all the factors that will come into play in that moment of reconsideration. Buyers reflect on the quality of their experience with the product or service. In the course of their valuing process, they take into account that a particular business has produced this enablement and either has offered a product or service that incorporates the qualities desired and envisioned at the outset, has failed to do so, or has even exceeded them.

When customers feel that the business has provided something of value, they acknowledge that the business has furnished them with a product that makes the experience worthwhile. A customer's decision to repeat the purchase when the product is used up affirms the business's efforts. A relationship is now established between a business and a customer in fact.

2. Value strategy focuses on generating, establishing, and maintaining the enduring and prospective aspects of the buyer's experience with enablement and the product.

A single sale does not create value until, and unless, it leads to the establishment of a relationship based on the desirability or necessity of the enablement and its product or service. A sale, at the moment of exchange, only sets up the condition in which a value relationship has the potential to develop. This observation flies in the face of conventional strategic thinking, which assumes that a business can autonomously make

Figure 3.1
Value Versus Consumption

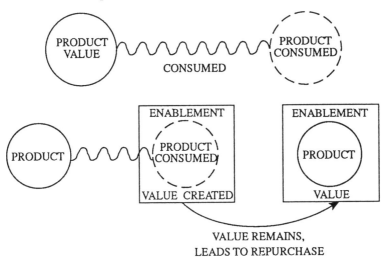

VALUE REMAINS,
LEADS TO REPURCHASE

decisions that lead to sales, market share, and profits or can create needs that make sales inevitable. This kind of thinking directs strategy toward "capturing" what is assumed to be a viable and active market that is there for the taking. It focuses its attention on the procurement phase of the process, or the deal in the transaction.

Value strategy, however, is directed at meeting all the requirements that *precede* the purchase in the prospection and projection phases of the buying decision and that follow on the purchase in the enablement stage of the transaction. A value-based strategy appeals to the *qualitative* components of the experience of the buyer and solidifies a positive, affirming impression of the experience. The initial sale is only the beginning: The aim of value strategy is to extend that initial action into a relationship and then to widen (by means of reputation, imitation, and emulation) that base of relationships.

Hence, our buyer is not merely a "consumer." Consumption is tied to the idea that a product is used up in the course of its fulfilling a need. But if, as we have said, the value concept points to enduring aspects of buyers' orientations toward meeting life requirements, the value of an enablement (as distinct from the features and benefits of the product or service itself) is not used up. The value of a product or service is only established when buyers are willing to return to it again and again (see Figure 3.1).

As we understand and view the term *value*, even as one uses up a product and consumes it, the value of the enablement is not extinguished or consumed along with it. To the contrary, in consuming the product, the value is reinforced and solidified and points to its continued vitality. Presumably, the buyer will want to replace that specific product and repeat the product-enabled interaction when the need arises. Consumption just sets up the situation in which a product will have to be purchased repeatedly in order to continue to participate in that activity.

The value process constantly and continually points beyond any specific situation that is happening now and points to the future—to images and ideals and to other products that enhance a buyer's life and world. The critical component of the value relationship is the buyer's expectation of being able to continue the activity by there being a continued supply of product. A one-shot purchase does not create value.

A business is involved in creating value when people count on interacting with their world in certain ways be means of this product *and* when other people channel their energies and resources to meet that demand. The aim of a strategy that leads to creating value is not to make a product that is purchased, used, and consumed—that only generates a one-term return. The aim of value strategy is to establish the buyer's rightful expectation that he or she can interact in his or her world in a certain way that completely depends on this product or service, now and in the future.

But this also means that strategy can no longer conceive of customers as composing "market share." As far as the customer is concerned, there is nothing in the dynamic of the value process that makes it necessary to buy any particular item. For one thing, a customer is not merely satisfying a need that repetitiously arises again and again. The value of a product evolves over time, and the choices that are available to meet the projections that the new value process requires have also evolved. Each customer is a new customer, even if the individual is a repeat customer.

3. Value strategy seeks to establish a long-term relationship with customers.

Short-term gimmicks, lowering prices, adding or giving away amenities, or other techniques to drive up sales, for instance, have nothing or little to do with creating value. They may generate sales to launch a product or to keep one afloat during a time of transition, for instance. And while sales in the short term are necessary, they are not sufficient to establish the value of the enablement or the product that supports the enablement.

Value strategy establishes and solidifies relationships that can be sustained over long periods of time in such a way that people are likely to seek out and be willing to incorporate these enablements in their lives. Still, value strategy is maintained only by continual focus and effort in the here and now. It is a strategy that is short on words and promises and long on ensuring the full presence and energetic carrying out of actions that support these key relationships.

Thus, value strategy has an essentially constructive and affirming outlook on the role of business and the economy in general. It has little interest in catering to consumer maladies that degrade experience, choice, and personal integrity.

For instance, materialism (or consumerism) is a kind of dysfunction in which people mistake the mere fact of possessing things or money for the interpersonal, spiritual, and societal qualities of life. If we think about it for a moment, it is easy to see how materialism degrades the value relationship. Without getting on a soapbox to preach, we can understand how materialism usually results in a pointless and inconsistent accumulation of things in people's lives.

Consumers end up with attics or closets full of things often forgotten— and certainly not used. From the business's point of view, materialism generates initial sales but little else. In terms of the value relationship, then, materialism creates distractions and actually limits the ability of the business and the buyer to integrate the product into wider frames of reference that can enhance the activity for the buyer and ultimately lead to opportunities for a business to carry out enhancing innovations.

There is another consumer malady that is even more personally debilitating and destructive to establishing a value relationship. I call it *immanent emptiness*, a malaise of contemporary life that is marked by a feeling of helplessness and emptiness in the face of the swift pace of changing mores and superficial life-styles. Being overwhelmed by choices, by advertising messages, and by the appearance of there being a product for every ill and lack, people lose track of their inner moorings. They get cut loose from the lasting and enduring relationships with other people, their community, and the world that give their lives real meaning. They mistake the messages of the advertisers for a real message about how to live and make decisions in one's life.

This malady degrades the value relationship because it leads to disillusionment and cynicism. Ultimately, no product or service will provide people with a sense of self-worth and connectedness to the things around them. And without those connections to other people, to communities, to nature, I think we can agree, there can be no lasting sense of fulfillment or joy. If that is the case, a business cannot provide products or services that will contribute meaningfully to their lives either. Thus, a cynicism about business and what it provides arises, precluding any possibility of establishing a constructive and supportive value relationship.

Value strategy has no need to prey on these degraded forms of material dependency. Premium beer makers, for instance, are not dependent on alcoholism for their ongoing success. Companies that recognize the destructive effects such forms of material dependency have on their ability to create value even use their advertising resources to heighten awareness about the consequences of abuse stemming from use of their products.

Efforts like these, however, are not entirely sincere in that they stem from the threat of governmental intervention. Campaigns such as those of beer companies to discourage excessive use of a product (even if it means fewer beers are sold in the short term) are examples of business's awareness of the limits of their place in people's lives. If brewers have instituted cautionary campaigns to fend off proscriptions such as those faced by cigarette manufacturers, so be it. The fact remains that decision makers recognize—or are made to recognize—that their success is tied to supporting constructive uses of their products and not to the short-term benefit of their inappropriate use or abuse. In terms of the value relationship, one restraining or positive norm-setting influence is as legitimate as another. The goal for business must be to provide opportunities for constructive, life-sustaining, communally supportive value relationships.

4. Thus, value strategy is also socially responsible and socially responsive.

We must acknowledge that there is a significant downside to our present economic system in terms of being able to provide for the safety, health, and well-being of everyone in our society. This has been evident since the sixteenth century when what is called the "enclosure movement" forced self-sufficient peasants off their land to a life of dependency, pauperism, and death in the early cities and towns of England. The writings of Charles Dickens and Karl Marx are testaments to the kinds of abuses that persisted even centuries later during the development of capitalism and the free market.

Although governmental regulation and a growing sector of enlightened business leaders have curbed many abuses these authors made famous, business decision makers today face questions about which products and services contribute in a positive and constructive manner to individual, community, and social life. These are not easy questions to answer. What is clear is that conflicts arise: between environmental standards versus living standards, or jobs, provided by the work; between short-term benefits versus long-term health risks; between local gain versus wider community harm, or vice versa.

These dilemmas, of course, extend into the arena of business ethics, which is not our focus here. But value strategy supports only those activities that sustain a society and the quality of life of its members. Selling drugs does not support a value strategy because drugs kill and debilitate their users. Selling shoddy merchandise does not support a value-based strategy because it degrades people's interactions and experiences. Conducting business in a way that pollutes or is contrary to standards of honor and integrity does not support a value strategy because all these things undermine the trust that people need as they venture into new arenas in their lives.

In other words, a business cannot long be involved in a commercial venture if its product flies in the face of community standards and social norms. As standards change—as people become more aware of the need to care for the environment, for instance, or of the cancer risks posed by hazardous materials—a business's value relationships will be affected accordingly. Practices once employed may become no longer acceptable. The value of controversial goods that for some have clear and pressing validity—such as logging or offshore oil drilling—is diminished by the presence of active and vocal dissent that negates the possibility of consensus or acceptance.

Ultimately, value strategy fully recognizes that business decision makers are responsible for social change and not merely passive observers or victims of the process. Thus, their decisions must be viewed in terms of their impact, their benefit or harm on the community at large. For instance, in one such dilemma of the early nineties, automobile manufacturers are being forced to consider, Even though it may cost more to build cars with air bags, is the industry promoting the right kind of social change (or hindering it) by not incorporating them into cars at a reasonable price? Changing social norms are factored into value strategy in such a way as to take account not only of their material costs but of their social benefit as well.

4

Turnover and the New World
of Business

VALUE AND MARKETS

As we saw, a value relationship is established when a buyer looks to a business to provide products that can be incorporated into a way of life or life-style. While we have described the complete, person-to-person relationship that leads to creating value, our understanding of the term *value* also includes the process by which the relative worth of something is determined. These determinations result from the activities that go on in a market.

In the prospection stage, the market may provide a cue or an incentive for making a particular commitment. In the projection stage, the market shapes and defines how the commitment would be fulfilled and makes it possible to narrow options down, or connect them, to the realities buyers face. The transactions that take place in the market determine the price of an exchange. Finally, because an array of options is discovered throughout the process, reconsideration and evaluation of the purchased product or service mark whether or not a specific product has any value at all.

As we know, for most businesses today, even for the most successful ones, the value process is not a story that ends "happily ever after." For many businesses, in technology, in consumer and business products and services, in pharmaceuticals and chemicals, there is a wrinkle that makes any outcome far more uncertain. The wrinkle is that people want new products. The value relationship does not satisfy constant, repetitious needs. People look to businesses to provide enablements that make it possible to maintain, enhance, or change the way they interact with people, institutions, and other products in their lives. Consumers look to businesses as the primary source for goods that satisfy their needs, but they also look to businesses as the source for creative thoughts, investments, and actions that will devise, present, and support activities about which we now can only dream.

Developments introduced by businesses have reshaped markets. On the most basic level, a *market* can be defined in a variety of ways: as a "collectivity of actual and potential buyers"; as a collection of businesses "supplying products that have some degree of suitability to the same potential buyers"; as "all people who buy or sell a commodity in the ordinary course of their affairs."[1]

But these are precisely the kinds of static images of the market that must be replaced. If what we say is true about the experience and trans-actions that lead to value, markets are far more volatile and turbulent than previously envisioned. Now a market encompasses *all the actions* that take place when businesses compete in order to establish whether or not their products and services will command or create any value at all. That value will be determined solely by buyers' responses to those products.

The good news in this is that because of the variability of buyers' demands and their receptiveness to innovations, many product ideas have a chance to establish themselves as viable, profitable, and value-creating enablements. Who would have imagined that people would flock to PCs or videocassette recorders (VCRs) and incorporate them so rap-idly and completely into their life activities? These developments show that the market does not set any limits, ideal or practical, on what en-ablements can gain favor.

However, for some businesses there is double-edged bad news in this as well. On the one hand, many items can claim a comparable worth. This means it is very difficult for a product to establish itself as a favored enablement. On the other hand, it means a business with a product that is already established has to look over its shoulder constantly to track, monitor, and anticipate developments that threaten its current position.

There are few extrinsic limits to introducing new products and new product categories. The technological appropriateness or even superi-ority of a product may be nullified by other market forces. This is what Sony experienced when its technologically superior Betamax video tape format was overwhelmed by NEC's competing VHS format.

For another, the time frame that any business has to make a success of a product is getting shorter and shorter. Even now, as the compact disk has just gained the status of being the quality standard for recorded music in the past few years, the digital audiotape format is making waves, and a new recordable minidisk is being prepared for market. This gives recording producers little time to recoup their costs for the changeover from vinyl disks.

TURNOVER

The primary way that the value process affects markets is to promote a climate in which changes to new products and enablements are supported, encouraged, or even demanded. As a result of this climate for change, constant upheaval becomes a structural element of that market. We witness this kind of thing in our lives all the time. It is a process we not only take for granted; we actually anticipate it. Trains give way to automobiles and superhighways; adding machines give way to calculators; typewriters give way to word processors.

But, as we know, these changes do not simply involve the introduction of one new product that affects one aspect of people's capabilities or means. The new product actually spawns other changes in people's lives as well. To grasp the extent of how a new enablement can produce dramatic changes in people's lives, let's perform a "thought experiment."

Pretend for a moment that two satellite photographs were taken at the turn of the century. In one photograph, we see a region in which there are just a few roads, and these would be mostly rutted dirt trails; housing is tightly concentrated, with a dispersion of farms and remote outposts around that center. In the second photograph, we see a region that has paved streets arrayed in a more extensive network; there are concentrations of housing in many locales, all connected by several roadways.

Somehow, the two regions in the photograph evolved in ways that differ in basic respects from one another. How did this difference come about? What enabled housing to spread out, and required smoother roads, was the presence of the automobile. One form of enablement, that of motorized personal transportation, had the effect of opening up new life-style opportunities (moving out of the city) and required the development of another (paved roads).

But the photographs do not show many other differences between the two regions. The automobile exerted an overpowering influence, generating new products (automobile insurance and, later, radar detectors) and new means of distribution (gas stations, aftermarket parts outlets) and reprioritizing existing facilities (making provisions for parking lots more important than sidewalks for walking between places). In the form of the mall, it created new contexts for buying; with the institution of consumer financing, it created new mechanisms to promote buying behavior; and in the form of mechanics, insurance agents, and mass production, it created new jobs, opening up new avenues for the application of human talents and abilities.

By comparing the two photographs, we observe the fact that a change in preference for a kind of enablement or enablement category changed the character of our daily lives. When this pattern became a generalized way to provide goods and services across many different kinds of products, from consumer appliances to the advancement of industrial machinery, the nature of markets and the forces that gave it shape and definition changed forever. In light of the fact that this phenomenon now occurs again and again, with ever greater frequency and depth of impact, the markets of today's world are driven by what I call turnover.

Market Style and Increasing Returns

Turnover refers to the fact that markets are continually reconstituted and reorganized by the conjunction or flowing together of many different factors stemming from the introduction of new enablements. Contributing to this incessant change are several factors:

- the tight linkage between science and industry that speeds product development, manufacture, and distribution;
- the increased availability of a variety of products, spurred by efficient and reliable international communications and transportation as well as stable international trade agreements;
- the increased affluence and the high levels of education achieved by many in industrialized countries;
- a sophisticated advertising industry that presents and depicts the benefits of new product offerings with alluring, captivating images;
- the increased governmental enforcement of consumer-mandated requirements (e.g., provisions for handicapped use and access; environmental responsibility; safety concerns); and
- the influence and effectiveness of privately organized and financed consumer advocacy.

A major contribution to formulating a revised model of market structure and development has come from the study of what economists call "dynamical, autoreinforcing or autocatalytic systems," systems that respond in unpredictable or chaotic ways to local stimuli before becoming "locked in" to a particular pattern.

In this view, as presented by W. Brian Arthur, when an innovation such as the VCR is introduced to the marketplace, and when the product is offered in competing formats, it is impossible to predict at the outset which format will ultimately succeed.[2] Arthur cites several examples in economic history, going back to the establishment of the Uccello clock of 1443, which was eclipsed a century later by the now-familiar twelve-hour clock, and then the VCR battle between Sony's Betamax system and the VHS system that eventually won out.

He shows why superior technologies that may actually present the best economic choice do not establish market dominance. He accurately describes how, at the outset, these kinds of markets are unstable and comprise "multiple equilibria" that can, over time, shape the outcome of a competitive situation in ways that could not have been predicted at the outset. According to Arthur, this happens by an accumulation of unpredictable, extrinsic events that result in small, incremental changes in consumer behavior. The accumulation of these small changes influences the choice of one format over the other.

To visualize this process, it is helpful to use a metaphor for change and motion developed by the science that studies chaos.[3] That science studies how orderly, regular, and predictable motion, at some point, gives way to chaotic, unpredictable gyrations. Even though these motions are random, leading to unpredictable outcomes, they do exhibit distinct patterns. Motion gravitates toward an "attractor"—a point or thing around which activity clusters. A vortex or "funnel" pattern is created around a significantly differentiated point in the field of motion. So while volatile motions within the vortex are unstable and a specific outcome of the motion cannot be predicted in advance, the vortex as a whole behaves in a relatively coherent way.

In our case, the automobile creates a point of differentiation in the personal transportation market that attracts a dizzying swirl of activity. A host of new products are made available to support and feed this enablement because businesses arise to meet the needs generated by the automobile. They create the "critical mass" of supporting products and services that establish the enablement in people's lives.

Large and well-capitalized businesses thus exert tremendous pressures to influence the outcome of the process. A story that illustrates this process occurred in the 1920s when the automobile market was stagnant, making no headway against competing technologies, such as light (commuter) and heavy (long-distance) rail. In response, General Motors, Firestone Tire, and Rockefeller's Standard Oil combined resources and purchased the rail system of the developing city of Los Angeles. Then, to create the conditions that would advance the automobile, they proceeded to rip up local rail systems and to replace trolleys with buses and to replace electric engines on the heavy rail lines with diesel-driven machines. The net effect of these actions was to establish the dominance of the automobile by eliminating rail as a viable contender for dominance as a preferred means of personal transportation in the Los Angeles area.[4]

New Product Hierarchies

Thus, in these highly volatile situations where new enablements and new products are introduced, the market is buffeted by two forces. On the one hand, it is allowed to be disrupted because consumers accept new enablements or ways of doing things that are supported by the products and services businesses provide. On the other hand, the market becomes a battle between these free and highly competitive businesses that vie to establish their products as "attractor" or standard-setting enablements. These dual actions that take place in the market combine to determine whether or not a particular kind of activity will take place in people's lives at all.

Again, if we think of this situation in terms of our photographs, we have captured a time when an insurgent product moves into an existent market style and changes the mix of buyer requirements—or "turns over" one life-style in favor of another. In the area of personal transportation, this enablement creates what we might call a dominant or identifiable "market style," a *new hierarchy* among various options buyers have for ordering their lives and conducting their daily activities.

This hierarchy does not congeal solely as a result of buyers' dreaming of a better life. This hierarchy is also created by the efforts of businesses to provide the requisite range and variety of products that support a preferred enablement. To be sure, as we have already seen, buyers' preferences and proclivities play a role in opening the market up to new possibilities.

But in the final analysis, once an enablement has been established, buyers' choices of which enablements they use for the activities they engage in reflect the logic of the market style that mandates the incorporation and use of this enablement. People in this country do not buy cars only because they like them. Many people in fact do not like cars and/or driving. But the ways our communities are organized—the locations of stores, banks, and public facilities—require access to a car. In increments measured by one and then another product, a buyer is more or less compelled to participate in the market style at hand and in so doing, at the same time, supports and solidifies it in a particular form.

Returning to W. Brian Arthur's description of the market process, as these increments accumulate, the result is "increasing returns" to the makers of the attractor enablements. For one thing, they garner improved competitive position, thus increasing the consumer's incentive to buy the leading product. As the products and services that support a particular form of an enablement proliferate, that format takes on the mantle of being the standard. Think of the use of the term *Xeroxing* for the process of dry paper copying or *Kleenex* for naming disposable tissues.

Increased sales, profits, or returns then provide a company with the capital for additional, product development with which it can further strengthen its position. As Arthur points out, "The more people adopt a technology, the more it improves and the more attractive it is for further adoption. . . . A technology that improves more rapidly as more people adopt it stands a better chance of surviving—it has a 'selectional advantage.' "[5] This leads to a phenomenon he calls "lock-in," where a product does become firmly established, even to the exclusion of products with superior technology that are introduced later.

But establishing this advantage comes with a warning: "Early superiority, however," he warns, "is no guarantee of long-term fitness."[6] The same pressures that establish a market style lead, in time, to their overturning. The cycle intensifies as it encompasses more and more of the enablements that shape people's lives.

FROM THE TERRITORIAL MARKET TO ARENAS OF ACTION

In earlier times, market changes were precipitated by a few "natural" forces:

- changes in the availability of natural resources, climate, or cataclysms;
- population and demographic changes and shifts;
- changes in the flow and/or concentration of capital;
- technological innovation, either on the production side or on the consumer product side; and
- governmental intervention or changes in geopolitical situations.

Accordingly, the image of market change was evolutionary. Changes were thought to exert marginal pressures on *existing* products in such a way as to affect price and profits but to leave intact the way in which they satisfied needs and the priority they had for people in their daily business and private lives. Accordingly, the markets that "contained them" remained constant and identifiable around these needs and priorities.

A market was a place in which all people, products, and money needed to make sales and satisfy needs were gathered together. Conceiving markets as "places"—as physical markets or as territories wherein competing companies vie for the same customer base—was sufficient.

But markets now face new and even more volatile forces. Turnover arises because any and all products in use are subject to a realignment in consumer preference, and priority, which can render it obsolete, nearly overnight. Three business actions that exert constant pressure leading to turnover are as follows:

- *Enhancement.* A product remains largely the same but is noticeably improved in terms of performance, convenience, or configuration. Examples of enhancement are the incessant changes in consumer electronics products such as microwave ovens (smaller sizes, easier to use) and home entertainment equipment (adding of remote control devices, easier programming, etc.).

  New products that open up new applications for familiar products are important factors here. The Sony Walkman, which allows for the playing of tapes on the go, and mobile telephones are such landmark enhancements. In time, they may lead to innovations that can be considered entirely new enablements.

- *Modification.* A product is substantially changed to meet new conditions or opportunities. The automobile has undergone many modifications in recent years such as pollution controls, safety modifications (antilock brakes, air bags), and improvements in engineering of the engine (four valves) and drive train (front-wheel drive). The sum of these product changes has actually changed the feel, character, and experience (not to mention the cost) of driving.

- *Replacement.* Products or entire enablement categories are replaced. The automobile's replacing rail systems has already been mentioned. Other striking examples are the replacement of the vinyl analog record by the digital, laser-read compact disk, the gradual replacement of moviegoing with home video watching, and the replacement of still or movie photography with home videos.

  With the growing power and momentum of these aspects of turnover, markets are now places of action, where constantly changing events create situations that must be responded to quickly and deftly. It becomes necessary to recast our image of markets in several ways.

1. Markets are no longer bazaars where wares are merely juxtaposed, set up against one another. With the proliferation of products available, people can closely match their prospective commitment to a well-developed enablement, making a change that is reasonable and intelligible and thus nonthreateningly feasible and even attractive. Markets, in this regard, set standards of expectations by means of which people assess their situations and make commitments to certain kinds of activities.

2. Markets are no longer places, actual or conceptual, where buyers and sellers meet to negotiate the price of the existing products that

are available. Markets are more like mental constructs existing in the minds of buyers and sellers. Information is disseminated through targeted systems of mail and telemarketing. The actual transactions take place in highly individualized settings: personal sales calls, telephone, modem, or mail. Access to the channels of communication (media, mail, telemarketing) and the effectiveness of those communications go a long way to determine what enablements and products will survive.

3. Of course, this means markets do not simply provide choice to satisfy needs. As we have said repeatedly, *markets foster, encourage, and promote change in people's lives.* To a buyer, the presence of a market in a category of products does not merely signify that something can be done in the here and now. It ultimately signifies that an enablement, along with the kinds of activities it supports, has a *future*, that some businesses will be paying attention to this way of doing things and will make its continuance and advancement possible and desirable.

The aim of the strategy we envision here is to ensure that a business will not only devote its energies to establishing a value relationship, will create value by means of this product-enabled activity, but that it will also be able to act effectively to meet all the expectations and ramifications of turnover. We will now focus on the kinds of actions that businesses have to undertake if they are to meet the challenge of turnover.

NOTES

1. Kjill Gronhaug and Hikhilesh Dholakia, "Consumers, Markets and Supply Systems: A Perspective on Marketization and Its Effects," in *Philosophical and Radical Thought in Marketing*, Firat, Dholakia, and Bagozzi, eds. (Lexington, Mass.: D. C. Heath, 1987), pp. 4–5.

2. W. Brian Arthur, "Competing Technologies, Increasing Returns and Lock-In by Historical Events," *Economic Journal* 99 (March 1989):10–13; also see the Bibliography for other entries by this author.

3. James Gleick, *Chaos: Making a New Science* (New York: Penguin Books, 1987).

4. Bradford C. Snell, "American Ground Transport: A Proposal for Restructuring the Automotive, Truck, Bus and Rail Industries," Testimony to the Subcommittee on Antitrust and Monopoly of the Committee on the Judiciary of the U.S. Senate, February 26, 1974, pp. 28–32.

5. W. Brian Arthur, "Positive Feedbacks in the Economy," *Scientific American*, February 1990, p. 98.

6. Ibid.

5

Creating the Market: Integration, Differentiation, and Competition

Turnover changes the rules of the marketing game. Business decision makers cannot assume that products or even enablements will remain viable for great lengths of time. Neither can they assume that their business will operate within relatively stable and long-lasting associations of competitors, buyers, and suppliers. And finally, just because a product has been made by no means guarantees that there will be a market for it.

Turnover-driven markets must be created and/or continually validated and revalidated. They are not just "naturally" there. Any strategy that deals with turnover-driven markets has to envision actions and decisions that address the whole range of transactions that have establishing a market as their objective.

Decision makers have to assume that there is no market for the product until the enablement is established as a preferred way of doing things with a wide segment of buyers. Thus, the business has to promote changes that support this enablement. And the business has to assume that it is the only source of information, training, and support for this enablement. Thus, each and every product offered has to be supported by the market-oriented activities of integration, differentiation, and competition.

INTEGRATION

Integration is the process of establishing the enablement in the life stream of potential buyers and of pulling together the resources and energies necessary to deliver goods to the buyer. Integration moves in two directions: integrating the *enablement category* and all the products that support and/or pertain to buyers' activities; and establishing the product's *domain*, or supplier, distributor, and other facilitating associations.

Establishing the Enablement Category

Integration is the set of activities that establishes an enablement category's *continuity*, its internal cohesion and viability, against the backdrop or within a matrix of already existing and accepted capabilities and enablements. A buyer's analytical vision of the market extends beyond any single entity to the plethora of entities, services, sales outlets, and delivery systems that compose and frame (or delimit and define) that market. Thus, it is to the advantage of the business to try to establish a new product within existing enablement categories. This allows the marketer to use terms, relations, actions, and activities that are already familiar to the prospective buyer.

The product category must be clearly delineated. Its purpose, application, and interconnection with other segments and life activities must be understood, known, and related to other aspects of the buyer's frame of reference. In the context of turnover, an unknown or not understood product is no product at all. Its value is zero. Correlatively, there is no market without the specific, compelling presence of a range of products that can support the enablement in a variety of buyers' conditions and circumstances. Companies that ostensibly compete within an enablement category will actually cooperate on some levels in order to accomplish this level of integration by, for example, forming associations and agreeing on technical standards.

Second, *distribution* must be well established in buyers' minds, and the supply must be sufficient for the demand level. The product must, above all, be accessible. But for distribution to be effective, people must have sufficient information about how the product and the enablement are made available. In the early stages of the value process, the market knowledge that is available is the rubric against which an individual projects his conditions and capabilities in relation to what is available to resolve the situation. Market information forms the basis of a buyer's ability to envision an enablement's adequacy accurately.

The Domain

To be viable, a business relies on other businesses, individuals, and associations that provide necessary goods and services that make its own actions possible. These include suppliers of equipment, materials, and labor, as well as service specialists, consultants, and professional groups.

Suppliers are deemed reliable when they help a business maintain a steady supply of its required inputs at stable costs (by enabling producers to achieve economies of scale, know-how, and efficiencies gained from experience) and when they provide an active network to help businesses achieve economies, efficiencies, and increased capabilities or expertise.

DIFFERENTIATION

Differentiation is the market-directed process that establishes a single product within an enablement category. Every company has to establish its own products and its own identity, and it does so by both positive and negative means. Positive means include steps such as advertising and informational programs that portray the product; negative means include the more "competitive" aspects of price cutting or distinguishing by other means including distribution, favorable financing conditions, or other ways that "beat out" another business's efforts.

Business's efforts at differentiation present all these product characteristics in a way that aims to reflect buyer preferences. Each product presentation attempts to emulate prospective buyers' frames of reference—income (purchasing power), commitment to the particular enabling interaction (creating high- and low-end product lines), and other facets of the buyers' life-styles. And then each product's "portrayal" is projected through informational channels to those buyers.

The viability and visibility of an enablement category can be measured in terms of the volume of different products within that category that are sold and the velocity of those sales. Yet this same volume and velocity can also lead to a phenomenon retailers call "hyperchoice," where too many offerings besiege buyers—even though the volume and velocity can be sustained. For instance, there are now two hundred cereals available in supermarkets,[1] and of the more than twelve thousand grocery products that were introduced in 1989, more than 80 percent failed.[2]

Modes of Differentiation

We have identified three modes of differentiation: (1) between different enablement categories, (2) between comparable, current products within an enablement category, and (3) between new and old products within an enablement category.

Businesses must establish the viability of their product against different categories of enablements. The market comprises far more in choices of enablements than any buyer will use in his or her lifetime. Buyers make selections as to which categories they will participate in. Simply, this means that buyers choose European vacations over a new car or buying a new set of skis rather than a new coat. This decision also expresses a preference for a kind of quality of life-style, a preference and/or judgment about priorities among different categories of enablements.

This mode of differentiation constitutes one element in the notion of positioning. In general, *positioning* is the process of a seller establishing in buyers' minds the quality of life they can have by using this product or service. In the context of differentiation among enablement categories, a seller seeks to establish where among competing priorities this enablement fits, who else (like the buyer) is involved with the product, and what else there is in the buyers' life-styles that accords with the enablement. The business's decision makers and representatives attempt to establish a position of priority, or a position that is close to an attractor that already does have priority.

The actions in achieving this mode of differentiation are more passive and informational in nature than the confrontational actions we shall see in the section on competition. The seller attempts to build a composite image of a particular set of interactions that require the product. The activity is to "show," "display," and "portray" likely outcomes when participating in this activity and then make these outcomes alluring and worth the expenditure. The specific features of the product itself are secondary.

The second mode is that of differentiation of current and comparable products within an enablement category. This reflects the buyer's careful evaluation of options and the comparison of those options available within that category to the resources that can be devoted to it. A high degree of choice within an enablement category, within fairly tightly defined price ranges, for instance, is a good indication of a mature market. A well-informed buyer can be more readily assumed for a mature market. Excluding some personally motivated and strictly adhered to brand loyalty on the part of the buyer, this battle is joined within a closed arena.

Again, the category of the automobile comes to mind. Not only are there more models and brands than ever to choose from; there are a mind-boggling variety of types of vehicles to choose from, a kind of vehicle to suit any life-style: sports cars for the young at heart; sports sedans for the young at heart with families; four-wheel drive "Wagoneer" type cars or small trucks for the adventurous; sedans, minivans, and station wagons for the family-minded; and good old gas-guzzling full-size sedans for still others.

As we have seen with this explosion of vehicle types, differentiation within an enablement category creates pressure to define the products to the most specific degree as a means to support a specific enablement and life-style. Each product has its advantages based on what it purports to accomplish, and each has its deficiencies. While this mode of differentiation leads to a measure of competition, in the larger picture, it actually supports the wide dissemination of the enablement category as a whole. The owner of the compact, fuel-efficient Honda Civic may look down her nose at the driver of the gas-guzzling Lincoln Town Car; but the fact is that they are both driving cars, supporting the automobile as the dominant enablement for personal transportation.

The third mode of differentiation, differentiation between old and new products within an enablement category, entails a one-way, irrevocable change in the character of the enablement overall. This follows from the fact that a new way of doing an established activity arises out of the aging or obsolescence of an existing mix of available enablements or from combining older features with innovations. The recent evolution of the bicycle comes to mind. The basic two-wheeled, leg crank-driven form is the same now as it has been for one hundred years. But advances in metallurgy in brake and gearing technologies have combined to create the new forms of racing bikes and the newer forms of mountain bikes and "hybrid" road bikes. These innovations have revitalized this venerable enablement category.

COMPETITION

In turnover-driven markets differentiation is seen less as a matter of competition than of comparison and juxtaposing one product against another. Differentiation, no matter how vigorous or energetic, ultimately has the effect of disseminating a core idea or enablement. On the level of value or enablement, differentiation is a constructive process that establishes the viability of the enablement and the products it requires.

There is no doubt that the race to integrate a market and differentiate one's product has competitive elements to it, as competition among automakers shows.

From the perspective of the value process, businesses must take account not just of horizontal market changes or substitute products but of vertical changes—changes as to how things are done, what enablements are brought into play and are judged to meet the expectations that are set during an individual's valuing process. Truly competitive strategies must contend not just with integration and differentiation but with turnover, or the ability of buyers to meet requirements from many sources and in many forms and combinations that change over time.

In value-based markets the truism is that even if an enablement category is essential (and outside of food, shelter, and clothing, few are), no product within a category is necessary. A buyer is not tied to any specific product for resolving requirements or realizing commitments and expectations. Thus, competition must be understood not just as a matter of differentiation but of survival of a mode of interaction.

Change constitutes a redeployment of the enablements people use in their daily activities. That means change constitutes a redeployment of the resources used in those interactions. True market competition, understood at its proper level of depth, is the battle to define the nature and quality of the experience the buyer will have during the activity for which the product is an enablement.

There are two crucial components to competition as we understand it. First, as we have seen, no enablement establishes itself without completing the entire circuit of both the experiential and transactional levels of the value relationship. Those circuits close only when the buyer fully perceives and believes that the enablement provided during a current cycle of use will be available in its current or enhanced form when he is ready to buy once again. It is only then that the enablement is established and the daily life activities it supports are conceived and envisioned in the specific ways the product makes possible.

Competition must be seen as a process of fully grasping and fulfilling the terms by means of which the enablement is used and understood by its users. The deeper and more complete the understanding, the more competitive the business will be.

People choose IBM computers, for instance, not because they are easier to use than Apples (which they are not), not because they are packaged in the most attractive and convenient forms (as of this date, IBM still does not have an affordable lap top), and not because they employ the latest technology (Compaq and others have staked out the territory of technical innovation). IBM commands its market because of the fact that people know (or believe so strongly) that IBM will be around when it is needed for service support, expansion, and upgrades. They appreciate and buy into that company's role in ensuring the viability and applicability of personal computing.

On the other side of the coin, however, U.S. automakers lost market dominance on their home turf because they lost the battle of advancing the experience of driving. The Japanese and Europeans develop automobiles that correspond to what people want and expect from driving, including mileage, reliability, and durability, including the fit of the parts (no rattles), the characteristics of handling (front-wheel drive), and styling. The U.S. automakers have yet to come to grips with this depth of the relationship car owners have to their experience of driving and their relationship with the companies that meet their requirements.[3]

Second, no enablement exists but for the efforts and decisions of the business that brings it about. All aspects of the product are called into play: its attributes, quality, means of delivery, ease of incorporation, and price. Thus, the terms of competition are not defined by business's actions aimed at integration or differentiation at all. The parameters are set to some extent by the business's material resources, but mostly they are set by a company's will to meet its customers' requirements.

The U.S. automobile industry did not lose its edge because it lacked resources, or because it did not have the ability to make quality cars. It lost its edge because it built cars to satisfy accountants' balance sheets and lost sight of building cars that people wanted. It lost the ability to build smaller, quality cars profitably because, for decades, it was able to realize profits by protecting market share and keeping prices high while not innovating and improving either the production process or the end product. As Bradford Snell points out, prior to the seventies the U.S. automakers only innovated when governmental intervention forced safety modifications.[4] Their loss of prominence was predestined by their own definitions of how people viewed and experienced their products. They were wrong.

To compete in a turnover-driven market, decision makers must go beyond mere differentiation from the pack of existing products and tackle the more challenging job of "creating value." They must drive their companies to provide enablements that contribute to the quality of activities in people's daily lives. In the final analysis, competition in value-based markets is a matter of organizing resources and maintaining the focus necessary to participate in a viable and growing value relationship.

Writers such as Michael Porter, or marketing-oriented writers such as Theodore Levitt, use phenomena such as image, features, and price as targets for actions that are supposed to contend with these market forces. Our point is that these actions might be effective if markets and products were based on satisfying repetitious needs that are met by the same product or variations of that product. For a time, these actions are certainly necessary for differentiating products within an enablement category, but in turnover-driven markets, they are not sufficient for dealing with true world-class competition.

The value process, based on conscious choices among socially available options, promotes the ability of a person to engage the world by means of an enablement. Since so many companies answer the call to provide products that support an enablement, there are too many factors and contenders in play. The value process is an inherently open concept. It permits too much variety of product and product combinations for these closed "competitive" strategies to be effective.

In another variation of the classical strategy, the *portfolio* school prescribes variations on horizontal or vertical integration as a means to contend with destabilizing forces. The idea is to erect "barriers of entry." But in these days of true international competition, a barrier any business can erect ends up being as effective as the Maginot Line was against

German planes and tanks. Again, these portfolio strategies would be effective if markets were generally fixed in terms of the players involved and in terms of the enablements that meet the requirements for their customers' interactions. One could acquire a quality company that supported either the production or end application of a product and be home free.

Turnover, however, proscribes the effectiveness of this strategy. Today's quality company may be tomorrow's dog if new market styles develop that are beyond the pale of the existing portfolio. IBM's recent experience with Rohlm is an example of the failure of this approach. IBM purchased the telephone networking company in the mideighties, thinking it would provide a basis to compete with the newly independent AT&T (which had designs of attacking the personal computing enablement). But communications technology evolved in a way that didn't support the Rohlm-IBM connections, and the computer giant sold its shares at a loss.

NOTES

1. "Free Choice: When Too Much Is Too Much," *New York Times*, February 14, 1990, p. C1.

2. "New Products Clog Groceries," *New York Times*, May 29, 1990, p. D1.

3. "A New Era for Auto Quality," *Business Week*, October 22, 1990, pp. 82–96.

4. Bradford C. Snell, "American Ground Transport: A Proposal for Restructuring the Automotive, Truck, Bus and Rail Industries," Testimony to the Subcommittee on Antitrust and Monopoly of the Committee on the Judiciary of the U.S. Senate, February 26, 1974, p. 12.

6

Position, Profit, and Strategy

Turnover-induced market instability increases the risks a business must assume in two ways: First, businesses must continually face risk in the form of offering innovations and new products that may or may not take hold with buyers. Second, turnover exerts tremendous pressure on the business to realize the highest profitability possible within the shortest possible time frame. This greatly increases the risk incurred with each venture, since there is little time in which an investment can be recouped.

But profit, as we shall see, is not a right the business has earned just because it makes products or delivers services. To the contrary, the worth and value that translate into profit must be proved and justified with each sale and with each enabling transaction. Strategies must be directed at the efforts that meet those daily challenges. Thus, a value strategy also envisions a new understanding of how prices are maintained and profits earned from sales.

POSITION AND PROFIT

The value process traces a buyer's decision to leverage present resources in anticipation of an enhanced quality of life in the future. Buyers assign a priority to a particular enablement and will commit resources in order to purchase this enablement that is adjudged to increase, further integrate, and/or enhance their life activities in the future. The higher the priority assigned to this item, the higher the premium that buyers will assign to the enablement, the more willing buyers will be to pay a high price or commit substantial personal resources to the product.

Profit thus signifies buyers' preferences for enablements and products under specific circumstances such as current market mix, level of technology, and prevailing social norms. Buyers realize that continuing to have the product available means the business incurs risk by redesigning and retooling, making mistakes, and fending off hostile market or asset raiders. But when the enablement is assigned a high priority, buyers feel that a premium in price over the cost of production is justified.

But how much profit are people willing to provide? That depends on what we call an enabling product's *position*. Profit first reflects an enabling product's position in a hierarchy of buyers' life-style requirements. Second, it reflects the product's proximity to an "attractor" or core technology in a product category or market niche. A buyer will pay tens of thousands of dollars for a car because it is regarded as (and has been so well integrated into the Western life-style that it is in fact) essential. Oil, insurance, radar detectors, and a host of other products likewise maintain their prices based on the automobile's success as an attractor enablement.

In general, an attractor or core technology is able to command a very high rate of profit. The closer a product is to that attractor, the more it can share its "aura," so to speak, the higher the profit it can command. Oil was always somewhat valuable in an industrial society, but with the advent of the automobile as an attractor enablement and core technology, it assumed the mantle of "black gold."

A product's position signifies its proximity to an attractor product or core technology and a high, or at least a reasonably stable, place in the hierarchy of enablements that buyers require and/or esteem. Prices can be protected and profits maintained because the enablement has assumed a role of importance in people's lives such that they are willing to pay a premium price in order to have that enablement.

Since profit is dependent on the rate and outcomes of turnover, a product's viability—its profitability—is also circumscribed within a time frame that is strictly limited by the forces of enhancement, modification, and replacement as we saw above. The rate of profit any particular product enjoys is subject to a profile that resembles the classical bell-shaped curve (see Figure 6.1). In its incipient stages, of introduction and integration, risks are high and profits are low, even when prices are unusually high, as a company has to muster its energies to establish its specific concept of the enablement that the product executes. A higher level of profit is possible (with or without price decreases, depending on its position vis-à-vis the attractor or core technology) once the product category is established, risk is put behind, and comparable products are few.

Figure 6.1
Profit Bell Curve

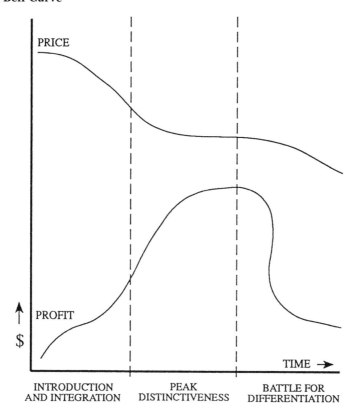

PRICE

PROFIT

$

TIME →

INTRODUCTION   PEAK   BATTLE FOR
AND INTEGRATION   DISTINCTIVENESS   DIFFERENTIATION

MARKET HISTORY

When the product enters the stage when it must battle to differentiate itself from among many comparable products, the pressures on prices and profits increase markedly. Classical strategies are often directed at this stage of the product life cycle, focusing on extreme efforts to protect prices and maintain profits against "replacements" and "new entries" into the market. But classical strategies make a crucial error in the face of turnover at this juncture. They mistake their efforts at differentiation within an enablement category for being a struggle to maintain position and hence profitability.

Differentiation is not the true source of profit. On the contrary, differentiation, in any of its forms, pits costs against profits. These costs are necessary because a product is so well known and estab-lished that the enablement can be tailored to ever more refined and segmented applications and situations. When the term *position* is used by advertisers and conventional marketers, they are referring to this process of finding, creating, or congealing a product's proper market niche.

In the context of turnover, when a product is so well established that differentiation is the primary battleground, its profitability has already peaked, and the product category is ripe for change, at least in the form of enhancement or modification, if not replacement. This is what we witnessed in the automobile market in the sixties. U.S. carmakers, following the strategies of Alfred P. Sloan, waged endless battles for market share based on styling differences and brand loyalties.

However, as we have seen during the past twenty years, no barriers to entry were sufficient to keep out the well-capitalized Japanese and European carmakers who enhanced automobile technologies with high mileage, well-assembled, and superb-handling (front-wheel drive) cars. Turnover struck the Big Three. As they and other industries have discovered, when a stage of market development is reached wherein a product category's profits must be protected by "artificial" means such as price fixing or protectionist trade barriers, that enablement category (or the segments of the industry that require such protecting) is often past its stage of peak profitability and, in some cases, may actually be moribund.

Thus, in the context of turnover, the strategic source of profit is position, or proximity to the core technology and/or market style that acts as the defining and standard-setting form of enablement. So the factors that determine profitability in the environment of turnover transcend the product itself. A product's profitability ultimately reflects the business's ability to project its leadership in the process of change and in the ongoing development of the product category as a viable enablement. The true battle for the position that leads to profitability is the drive to establish and distinguish useful and meaningful enablements—and nothing less.

TURNOVER AND THE STRATEGY
FOR PROFITABILITY

This conception of how profits are derived has radical consequences for strategy. In the context of value-based markets and turnover, profits can no longer act as the solitary and motivating goal of business. In a value-based market, profits cannot be predicted or assumed as an outcome of a business's actions.

Profits now assume a different status, one that is no less critical than what classical strategies envision but one that makes profit an operating imperative rather than an end in itself. Profits become a basic, compelling, and irreducible necessity of the business's survival, in a way analogous to how breathing is an absolute necessity. But just as breathing is not regarded as the goal of human life, profit cannot be the sole, motivating goal of a business. A business simply cannot pursue its goal if it does not have profits with which to meet the incessant demands of turnover and change, but neither can decision makers pursue goals that have immediate profits as their envisioned end.

Profits could more reasonably act as a goal when market and production conditions were different. In the classical literature, profitability is accounted for by supply and demand or market share strategies. These strategies were based on the observation that goods and services were provided that satisfied definable needs, that they remained more or less constant over long periods of time, and that the goods involved had to be purchased again and again to satisfy the reemerging need.

In supply and demand models, profitability stems from a business's (or an industry's) ability to meet demand in the context of scarcity. A strategy prescribes either benefiting from the fact of scarcity or creating the impression of scarcity in order to drive prices up. Sustaining profitability depends on maintaining that impression.

Market share strategies promise profitability when companies have a commanding position of power over a few known competitors in a relatively stable market and use that power to maintain and defend a profitable price. Commanding a sizable market share allows a company to maintain profitability by leveraging higher, defendable prices against the lower costs it gains from both economies of scale in the use of equipment and the flattened learning curves of its labor force. Strategy here dictates defending that market share—defending against "substitute products," against additional product entries, against social developments that change or diminish the ability to control those markets.

But people's buying motivations as well as their orientations to markets in the context of turnover are quite different than those presented in the classical models. In the value-based conception, markets have no other purpose than to provide enablements. There is no absolute need, no benchmark, standard, or compelling necessity at work here to elevate one product over another or to vouchsafe any market. So while the factors of supply and demand and market share can be valid measures of a product's performance within limited time frames, they do not necessarily correlate to the level of profit a product can command in the market over the long term.

Thus, value strategy has a different orientation toward markets than classical strategies. Classical strategies use markets in order to gain profits and return on investment. A value strategy regards a market as being beyond its control—and so regards it as the set of dynamic conditions and relationships out of which profits will either be made or not by virtue of the success a business has in providing meaningful enablements.

The enablement and the product that supports it, including all the elements of the product that make the enablement a worthwhile and valued experience for buyers (i.e., the product's quality, intelligibility, pricing, and service as well as its compatibility with standards and norms of prevailing social requirements), are the focus of attention. The bottom line determines how much effort and material can be brought to bear on the challenge; and subsequently, a firm's profits may indicate the potential for success of a venture. But the role of providing enablements for people to use and value in their lives comes first if any venture is going to succeed.

1. Value strategy meets demands that ensue from the efforts needed to provide specific enablements, not from the business's internally defined capabilities.

Several writers have warned companies to build on their internal competencies rather than stray off into the conglomerate-type thinking of a Harold Geneen (ITT Corporation) or even of Henry Ford, where the drive for capital and control lead to excesses of horizontal or vertical integration. Here, we have a slightly different slant on the subject.

Our concern is that turnover splinters and fragments mass markets into *micromarkets* where smaller groups of people use products that suit more specific situations for more limited periods of time.

There are at least two forms that micromarkets assume. On the consumer level, micromarkets are marked by the proliferation of product configurations and price ranges. The food industry, for instance, has seen this evolution as supermarkets carried nineteen thousand different items in 1989, up from fourteen thousand in 1985.[1] Even basic staples such as milk are now marked by this proliferation and specialization. A milk producer does not just homogenize milk but produces a "menu" of products, from homogenized vitamin D whole milk to low-fat or low-lactose to various skimmed-milk varieties. Each of these products appeals to its own micromarket—defined by buyers' life-style requirements—and has several competing producers in it.

Another form of micromarket is that of the specialized producer of goods or services, where there are few customers in fields that are nevertheless supported by and within their own markets. These micromarkets or market niches are prevalent in technical industries, for instance, where a few producers of key products, such as semiconductors, need to be supported by specialized suppliers. Again, several competitive companies vie to supply the few available customers within this niche.

The development of micromarkets weighs heavily against the idea of integrating a company in either a horizontal or vertical manner in order to meet mass market demand. Mass market demand that is present in the incipient stages of a product's or product category's existence will inevitably splinter and fragment into micromarkets as people become more familiar with the enablement and as more companies enter the field of production. Value strategy therefore deepens and focuses the resources with which decision makers address the requirements of the company's micromarket. In responding to its troubles during the past few years, IBM, for instance, decided to break up into separate, smaller companies.

Using value strategy, a business will address the proliferation of micromarkets by acquiring and concentrating resources in a way that strengthens its focus and capabilities to enhance its enabling product or service. It will also exert its energies in such a way that its customers know that this effort is being made. This aspect of strategy demonstrates and validates the business's commitment to the value relationship that makes the enablement viable in the first place and desirable in the long run.

2. The marketing component of value strategy hinges on the duration and volatility of the product life cycle.

Thus, markets must be conceived less as being territories to be defended than as clocks that mark out the time of the effective life of an enablement and its products. That effective life is determined on the microlevel by the individual buyer's transaction with and use of the product and on the macrolevel by the total aggregate demand (or customer base usage) for the product.

The *micro*interval of the buyer's transaction combined with the *macro*interval of aggregate demand determines the *rate* of change a business must contend with or the product's life cycle. The interplay of micro- and macrointervals works this way: The transactional microintervals determine the frequency with which reconsiderations of the product's value take place (see Figure 6.2). In some cases, such as that of advanced technology production equipment, the equipment might last longer than the demand for it, the pace of product development being shorter than the equipment's effective life. In this case, where a buyer is looking for the opportunity to depreciate the older equipment and invest in newer technology, a simple service call might precipitate reconsideration and a new value process. All the forces that bring on turnover exert their influence at these points of reconsideration; so a repurchase may or may not take place at that time.

The duration of the transactional microinterval thus determines the time span over which a demand macrointerval may occur. For example, a maker of a popular cereal deals with weekly transactional microintervals, but the effective macrointerval for the business is extended by as much time as aggregate demand allows. If other turnover-inducing influences are weak, the aggregate demand may hold. If

Figure 6.2
Micro- and Macro-Intervals in Buying Decisions

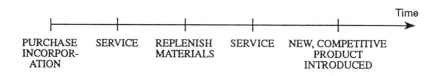

MICRO-INTERVALS:

POINTS OF RECONSIDERATION THAT
CAN TRIGGER A NEW PURCHASE

                                                                          Time

PURCHASE	SERVICE	REPLENISH	SERVICE	NEW, COMPETITIVE
INCORPOR-		MATERIALS		PRODUCT
ATION				INTRODUCED

MACRO-INTERVALS

                                                                          Time

ESTIMATED PRODUCT LIFE   NEW PRODUCT OR
                                          NEW PRODUCTION
                                               DEMAND
                                                *
                                              NEW
                                            PURCHASE

those influences are strong, transactional microreconsiderations may go in a negative direction and aggregate demand may fall precipitously as weekly decisions steer reconsiderations toward repurchases of other products.

Markets must now be conceived as dynamic and changing arenas. The forces marketing strategies must contend with are results of local and variable value relationships that are irrevocably influenced, changed, or even made extinct by the actions of businesses in the micromarket (or enablement category) and the decisions of their customers. The strategy must incorporate an innovation schedule into product planning that reflects the (micro) transaction and (macro) aggregate demand rate of turnover.

The style of market research, therefore, has to be less quantitative in terms of numbers of customers and their locations than it is descriptive of customers' understandings and expectations with regard to the product. In narrative form, research describes those aspects of the customers' experience with the product as an enablement and what aspects of that experience create enthusiasm and loyalty and define quality.[2] A principal element of value-based marketing strategy is to devise feedback loops that give precise soundings of how well the enablement is faring as a mode of interaction between and among customers. Market research is not a matter of the raw numbers—how many customers possess the product. The key, value issues are the rate at which people incorporate the products into their lives, the status they assign to them, and the rate at which they reconsider the product for renewal and/or replacement by means of repurchase.

It is crucial to know how and when influences such as technological trends, demographics, income, and education levels will start to affect buyer decisions. The intention is not merely to erect barriers or offer new features but to plan for in-depth and meaningful innovation in a timely and orderly way.

3. The market-oriented effort must ensure that all components of the product and product category's integration and differentiation are communicated and firmly established in the consumers' minds.

Since classical strategies are based on the conception that products satisfy constant and repetitious needs, they make the logical assumption that the need or interaction that it pertains to is a given, beyond the pale of the business to address. Business's profits simply come from selling products or services. While this may have been true for most products in earlier times, and may be true for some raw material products today, this assumption applies to fewer and fewer of today's business products.

Today's products involve technologies, materials, behaviors, and interactions that in some cases were not even conceived as recently as ten years ago. The parents of children who play Nintendo games will attest to the skills (or new combination of skills) that their children possess that they do not. Many of the products now commanding profits and creating value are completely new. The markets and domains for them had to be established from scratch—including education, new channels of distribution—and ancillary and supporting products also had to be established.

New technologies often affect even traditional products—the way microwave ovens have changed the packaging and presentation of foods comes to mind. The attentive service these businesses pay to the process of establishing their enhancement has the rippling effect of creating buyer expectations of how businesses should behave in general. This creates new pressures and standards of integration. For instance, people begin to expect that they will be able to sample products or that companies will offer coupons.

Thus, marketing in value strategy involves a complete grasp and understanding of all the elements required to sell the product and also a complete grasp of the elements needed to establish, maintain, and enhance the transactions that support it. This means the business strategy must envision all the activities required for providing information, access, maintenance, and renewal about the product and how it performs as an enablement.

4. Profitability reflects the business's commitment to leadership and its ability to guide and shape a product-enabled activity, rather than its ability to defend the turf it had occupied in the past.

All strategies stress the all-important buzzword *innovation*. But the term has a different weight in the context of turnover-driven markets. In classical strategies, innovation is a defensive strategy, aimed at keeping market share and protecting profits and margins already attained in a market. The intent of this level of innovation is differentiation of products within established enablement categories such as transportation, consumer electronics, prepared foods, and computers.

In the face of turnover, however, no market is secure. In this case, it is especially true that offense is the best defense. Decision makers must define and shape the enablements by means of which people interact with their world. It means exerting the complete effort and commitment necessary to ensure that buyers can engage their world with this enablement now *and* that the product-enabled interaction will be supported and enhanced in the future.

A business strategy that takes turnover into account must be based on the assumption that it is not dealing with a market that is characterized by stability and diminishing returns. Volatility is the condition that strategy must address so that its efforts at establishing the enablement and its products will meet with increasing returns.

Acquisitions can be used to improve the ability of a company to compete at the level of value, and there are many examples of enablement-enhancing mergers and acquisitions:

- The purchase of Apollo Computer provided Hewlett-Packard with the ability to enter the workstation market by enabling companies with complementary products to synergistically enhance or establish the viability of a product category.

- Ford's purchase of Jaguar enhanced or improved the viability of the luxury car product category by providing a quality carmaker with capital and an extensive dealer network.

- Sony's purchase of Columbia Records and Universal Studios provides Sony "software" or material to be used on its hardware products, and it provides the record company with a partner in making its material available on state-of-the-art equipment and formats.

- General Electric's purchase of RCA enabled both companies to achieve an appropriate scale of operations in taking on world-class competitors such as Matsushita and Philips.

Of course the ultimate purpose of strategy is to establish and maintain leadership in one's enablement category. No amount of market tinkering or restructuring and acquisition will help unless a business is willing to take on change, with all its implications, including changes needed to its own identity and ways of doing things. The kind of orientation and actions that are necessary will be the focus of attention in part II, where we fully delineate the characteristics of the organization that can operate successfully in the new world of business.

NOTES

1. "New Products Clog Groceries," *New York Times*, May 29, 1990, p. D1.

2. See Gareth Morgan and Linda Smircich, "The Case for Qualitative Research," in *Marketing Theory: Distinguished Contributors* (New York: John Wiley, 1984); and C. J. Thompson, W. B. Locander, and H. R. Pollio, "Putting Consumer Experience Back into Consumer Research: The Philosophy and Method of Existential Phenomenology," *Journal of Consumer Research* 16, no. 2 (September 1989): 133–146.

Part II

The Business

7

The Business Organization

THE LIFE OF THE BUSINESS

Because a business participates in a relationship specifically dedicated to providing enablements to buyers, we can make some basic assumptions about the conditions a strategy must always take into account:

1. The business exists because of demand for its product. A business exists only when it has customers making specific demands on it: No demand, no business. No business has a fundamental right to exist, except to meet demand, and no business exists when there is an absence of demand. Decision makers must assume that buyers using the value process are rarely tied to one brand or variety of product or service. What they are actually demanding is that a particular enablement they value be supported. Which business does this is immaterial as long as the demand is met.

The relationship between a buyer and a business is fundamentally unequal: Buyers are not dedicated to a particular value relationship—they use it. They choose to enter this relation to meet certain requirements, and they choose other types of relations for other things in their lives. When their transactions are completed, they leave the value relationship behind in order to get on with other things in life. Business, on the other hand, lives and dies by the success or failure of its value relationships with its customers. A business must elicit the demand for its specific product and make customers' expenditures of thought, energy, and money worthwhile.

This fact distinguishes the business as we understand it from the entrepreneurial firm or the start-up. A start-up is devoted to introducing and establishing an enablement for which there is as yet no demand, no preconceived expectations, no set parameters by means of which it is evaluated. The start-up is not created by demand but instead is the outcome of someone's as-yet-unproved insight. It does not create value until it becomes a business, until the time that people want to drive, mow lawns, write documents by means of the enablement its product supports.

The established business, in contrast, must successfully meet the demands of people who are already engaged in using this enablement. Its decision makers are acting within the context of an ongoing value relationship in which their business is being looked to as a solution and source for life-style requirements. The established business operates within the parameters of the demand that it has established. If decision makers lose their focus or will to continue, no one will be there to keep it alive. If the demand still exists, a competitor will gladly pick up the ball; if the demand doesn't exist, the absence will hardly be noticed. The business itself has the responsibility for making its actions needed and valued.

2. Putting all these factors together, one realizes that although a business exists because of demand, its actual work is to anticipate demand. The premise of the value process is that as customers use a product more and more frequently, they will integrate it more fully into their life patterns, enjoy the experience, and apply it to more areas of their lives.

So while demand for a product justifies or supports the existence of a business, the business has a future only to the extent that it meets the speculative aspect of demand, that it innovates and advances the product and its enabling qualities. The real task of business decision makers is to seek out, make decisions, and act on the basis of the opportunities they have to meet the envisioned demand in a timely, well-designed, and well-executed manner.

The decision makers put what they have successfully accomplished in the past at risk in order to create and/or perpetuate subsequent, similar, and/or enhanced products. They provide an enablement by acting as a buyer of labor, materials, services, and space in anticipation of what people will require in the future—fully realizing there is, concretely, no way of knowing whether or not that demand will be there when the product is ready to be shipped en masse.

3. The business exists as action. A business exists only by virtue of what it produces. What have you done for me today? is the real-life refrain of business life.

And the action of the business is also very specific. The action is always directed to the production of a *single* entity that is available for sale, that is, as a commodity to meet that demand. The entity may be a single product or a line of products or a distinctive service of some kind, but decision makers must ensure that the organization acts in such a concentrated and directed way that it satisfies the demands being made on it by customers.

That action is always shaped by markets. Markets compose the "rules of the game" for the business, and those rules change with the maturity of the market, the number of players, and the product. Decision makers must fulfill all the requirements of integration, differentiation, and competition that its markets dictate. Those requirements are specific to each enablement category and vary for each business, depending on its position within that category. Actions that fall outside those requirements may be successful, but they also run the risk of incurring the wrath of customers, suppliers, and competitors or simply not even being noticed because people are so accustomed to doing things in certain ways.

4. Businesses deal with or engender change. It is the province of bureaucracies to do things repetitiously, or to replicate the same actions again and again. Pressures from turnover and changing demand put businesses in the position not merely of being makers of things but of being decision makers about the nature of enablements. Not only do they determine the configuration of the products that support the enablement; they also work to extend their range and ease of use as well. Thus, businesses constantly undertake actions they have heretofore not taken.

Profit signifies that decision makers have taken advantage of opportunities and have established the enablement and its product as viable and even welcomed in people's lives. Growth means that the enablement is successful and that more and more people are adopting it as part of the way of doing things in their lives. Thus, demand increases, and the business must grow in order to meet that demand. Profits, or its capital, are the means a business has to grow and meet that demand and/or maintain its position as an enablement against other similar products or against other enablements.

5. Being a business decision maker requires a certain amount of motivation. There are two kinds of motivation that we think do not provide adequate support for being in business. The first is the goal of attaining personal wealth. While personal wealth is a compelling reason to own and run a business, it is not sufficient to sustain a person through the vicissitudes of business life. For one thing, in this day and age, the likelihood of getting rich in business is diminishing, not increasing. What wealth can be made will be greatly diminished by income taxes if not by feverish competition.

Another inadequate motivation is ego gratification: the goal of putting oneself in the upper tiers of society, hobnobbing with the stars, and gaining the adulation of peers. Keeping up such a life-style is what a *Business Week* cover story called "CEO Disease."[1] The story describes a chief executive officer's (CEO's) wish for ego gratification so strong that he (and it is men that are cited in this article) plunders the company, accumulating outrageous expenses while neglecting the day-to-day decisions the business needs. Many CEOs have been brought low by active boards or the bankruptcies born of such motivation.

Harold Geneen mentions the phenomenon of egotism as the leading disease of CEOs as well. He must feel sickened by much of what he sees in the way of CEO egotism, especially at his former company. When Geneen was hired by ITT in 1958, he accepted an offer of $125,000 in salary and no promises of bonuses or stock.[2] In contrast, ITT's board authorized a check for current chief executive Rand V. Araskog to the tune of $11.4 million in salary, bonuses, perks, and restricted stock, representing a 103 percent rise over 1989—all this while the company's return on equity had fallen to 11.5 percent in 1990 from 15 percent in 1980. According to pay consultant Graef S. Crystal, quoted in the *Business Week* article from which these facts are taken, this kind of action amounts to "a tremendous display of arrogance and insensitivity."[3] I am sure Geneen would heartily agree.

In the final analysis, the only motivation that truly sustains a business is the will of its decision makers to participate in a socially supported process of providing enablements that have an impact on people's lives. It may not be a pretty process, and people may get hurt along the way; the business may even fail eventually. But this motivation has the potential to sustain the drive and commitment necessary to deal with the virulent forces of life in the business.

The advantage of relying on the value relationship as a basis of motivation is that while personal rewards of wealth can also be there for some, a level of personal satisfaction can be attained by many. This satisfaction comes from fulfilling a dream and seeing it have a beneficial impact on people's lives. The value relationship is about a dream, after all.

The case of Steve Jobs comes to mind. He had (in his own words) more money than he could give away in his lifetime by the time he was involved in bringing out his Macintosh computer. His sole motivation, rather inelegantly executed in terms of managerial and interpersonal finesse, was to create a machine that would change people's lives. When he was dismissed from Apple because his irascible personality could not be tolerated in the ever more corporate culture (appropriately and of necessity) developed by its president, John Sculley, Jobs went off to start a new venture to fulfill another dream of social change. NeXT might not be as successful, but the motivation alone gives Jobs a chance to succeed at what others might not have dared to dream.

The most eloquent expression of this motivation for going into business life is contained in Matsushita's statement of purpose, written by Konosuke Matsushita, the company's founder. It sums up much of what this chapter attempts to express:

Happiness of man is built on mental stability and material affluence. To serve the foundation of happiness, through making man's life affluent with inexpensive and inexhaustible supply of necessities like water inflow, is the duty of the manufacturer. Profit comes in compensation for contribution to society. Profit is a yardstick with which to measure the degree of social contribution made by an enterprise. Thus profit is a result rather than a goal. An enterprise in the red will make all co-operating people poor, and ultimately the whole society poor. If the enterprise tries to earn a reasonable profit but fails to do so, the reason is because the degree of its social contribution is still insufficient.[4]

THE BUSINESS ORGANIZATION

Every business gathers in resources and then channels them through its organizational structure in order to produce a specific result. Every business is an organization. And because of the specific ways a business organizes itself, every business organization is unique. Even three businesses that produce similar products have distinct organizations. IBM, Hewlett-Packard, and Compaq all make computers that are highly competitive, yet their organizations are each quite distinctive. We have identified four factors that contribute to making each business organization distinctive and individual: mission, culture, capital, and management.

Mission

A business exists to meet the demand created by customers' use of its products. A business has a mission when it is committed to meet its customers' requirements and to participate in a value relationship by means of a concerted and organized action through its products and services. A useful and meaningful mission statement consists of four elements that together express the essential relationship between a business and its customers.

First, it names the company's field of action, including what products it makes (or what service it provides) and for whom. For smaller companies, this part of the mission can be stated very concretely and specifically, but larger companies will have to express it more broadly. For instance, Xerox Corporation defines its field as "document processing," which includes all products that are involved in producing, reproducing, transmitting, receiving, and storing documents. This goes far beyond the idea that Xerox makes copiers.

Second, the mission considers what this product or service enables their customers to do. This part of the statement answers the question, What is the value of my product or service to my customers? Another way to ask this question is, What does my product or service enable my customers to do that they would not otherwise be able to do? How does it enable them to achieve *their* goals? It conceives the product or service from the customer's point of view and includes the vision not only of the enablement itself but of how it connects or contributes to other parts of his or her life.

Third, the statement describes how the company carries out its operations with its customers. This is not a statement of platitudes, beliefs, and goals; it actually describes the actions that the company carries out to participate in a relationship with its customers. It includes standards, methods, and definitions of the organization but is not a listing of "positions," departments, or jobs.

Finally, the mission describes how the organization intends to respond to changes in that essential relationship. The business's mission must include an expression of how its role in that relationship is fulfilled and advanced and even defended in its environment. This can be an expression of how the organization's structure is flexible, or how its hiring and human resources policies support and encourage innovation. And it must include a plan for growth, especially as regards capital acquisition and allocation.

Culture

If businesses only made products, "culture" would not be an issue. Machines are capable of stamping out products, with little need for human intervention or, certainly, with no need for an organization. A business has a culture because it organizes people in such a way that they can collectively take up the business's struggle to survive in the context of its value relationships and/or strive to be a participant, even a leader, in those relationships.

Culture is a term that summarizes how the organization really relates to its stakeholders in general and its customers in particular. Edgar Schein defines culture as "learned responses to a group's problems of a group's survival in its external environment and its problems of internal integration."[5] We understand this to mean that culture is the set of understandings, assumptions, and precepts that binds individuals together into an organization so they can undertake decisions and actions in a unified, consistent manner.

The business participates in a relationship in which it makes enablements available according to the demands of customers who use its products or services. To do this successfully, the organization must embrace the meanings and expectations of the people who use the enablement and the supporting products and services it supplies. And since the value relationship is essentially an unequal one, it requires that the business to a greater or lesser degree take full responsibility for the success of that enablement. The organization has to take the initiative in that relationship.

Culture is expressed largely by the organization's policies, which are often written down, but an organization's culture really emerges out of the meanings and messages that arise at the seams of an organization's decisions and interactions. If a company espouses devotion to professional development but does not support continuing education—fires someone, for example, for neglecting overtime in favor of taking a job-related course in the evening—the cultural message is loud and clear: "Only the bottom line has meaning here."

Culture, in other words, mirrors the organization's value relationships in the way that it guides and controls or encourages certain actions toward those within and those external to the organization.

Culture is strictly a relational phenomenon of organizational life. Accordingly, it encompasses both the external and internal aspects of the organization's relationships. To highlight those aspects of a business's relationships that pertain most to developing a value-based strategy, we have identified three externally directed aspects of a business's relationships and four internally directed aspects. The three externally directed aspects of a business's relationships are:

- *Means*. To accomplish its goals and objectives, people in an organization will apply the means—methods, tactics, material resources—that the organization has determined are appropriate within its relationships. This application of means is limited only by the ethical considerations the organization accepts from its relationships. The people in the organization, in general, will try to meet the standards of conduct and apply the means regarded as appropriate by its customers.

- *Measurement*. Decision makers will measure the organization's performance according to the standards it recognizes as valid and meaningful for its markets (or, as we shall see, for whomever decision makers regard as its leading stakeholders). Decision points—including what thresholds indicate success or failure, what they choose as benchmarks against which to measure performance, what terms of analysis are used and in what combinations—frame expectations with respect to the validity, significance, and priority of people's actions.

- *Malleability*. However reluctantly, people in an organization will accept the level of change that its environment requires of them. A commodity producer working in a stable, unchanging environment will not need a culture that prepares for frequent, wrenching change and will not conceive of change as being a driving force in its strategy. An electronics producer, however, where change is driven by turnover, by rapid technical advance, and by international competition, will have to incorporate a strategy for change, the expectation of change, and the means to articulate meaningful scenarios for change. The question decision makers always face is how much initiative to encourage in this regard—how much to change versus what to preserve.

These four internally directed components of culture determine how well the organization will be able to carry out its intentions:

- *Words.* People in the organization develop a language and a communications style that express their perceptions of its essential tools, materials, expertise, and interpersonal relationships. These are reflected in factors of business life such as the protocols used in the routing of communications, in the level of formality or informality, and in the distribution of information—varying in quantity, frequency, quality, and content—to members in different parts and levels of the organization.

- *Walls.* Through repeated interactions, the organization develops protocols by means of which people in different areas of the company, and at different levels of the hierarchy, do their work. The quality and content of interactions at the boundaries of organizational departments and levels establish the invisible dividing lines among people, departments, and organizational levels.

   In their lowest form, boundary interactions degenerate into politics, where people defend "turf" against encroachment and change; in its highest forms, boundary interactions permit the application of different skills, perspectives, and insights during the course of change.

- *Wages.* Each organization develops its own means of allocating and controlling resources—monetary, material, and human. Controlling mechanisms (rewards and punishments, power and status, compensation, etc.) determine how decision-making capability and initiative are distributed among the members of the organization. Initiative is directly affected by the criteria used to distribute resources. When innovation and initiative are rewarded, it sends one message. When resources are directed toward enhancing trappings of power and bureaucracy that defend the status quo, it sends another.

- *Will.* The organization develops and articulates ideals that give meaning to and set expectations for daily interactions and operations. No matter what is stated in a human resources policy, day-to-day actions truly tell how well an organization respects individual initiative, how much it values the work people do, and how well it supports and builds on interpersonal relationships. The people in the organization permit and encourage interpersonal connections that either cross boundaries or constrain connections within them; they either support linkages of friendship and trust or do not.

We now move to the more analytical and judgmental aspects of organizational life as we consider capital and management.

Capital

A business is distinct from other kinds of organizations precisely in that it uses capital. Bureaucracies do not use capital; they use funds or revenues provided by other means to pay their ongoing expenses, and no more. Capital is required when new machinery is being purchased, when employees are being trained, and when products are being offered and there are not yet immediately known and confirmed buyers for them at the time of their production.

This is the situation faced by businesses in turnover-driven markets. Thus, we understand the term *capital* as being a means of payment for dictating new directions to providing product-enabled interactions. Capital comes from profits and is absolutely necessary. Profits are a result; converted into capital, they become a *means*.

Capital is used to seek out creative opportunities. It is a fund of resources that is designated to go into action, to participate in advancing and developing ongoing or new value relationships. Thus, capital is applied to a value relationship in its most speculative stage. Its application entails some knowledge—facts and figures pertaining to performance of the product category, historical knowledge and precedents, and so on; but it is primarily a relationship in which the capital's owner must decide what will transpire on the basis of his own judgment.

The decision to invest capital in a specific situation reflects a judgment about what this venture can bring about in the future. The judgment is based on an assessment of the personnel involved in the venture, their track record, knowledge, and drive to succeed. But the overall conditions of the society as a whole and its potential for being receptive to a particular enablement or product enter the picture as well.

Ideally, the more activities come under the sway of capital, the more new kinds of activities can be generated, supported, and even required. The result would be a life-style that has choice, variety, and differentiation in the kinds and levels of skills used in a society. Accordingly, to the extent that capital is not applied to value relationships in this way, society as a whole also suffers.

Capital consists partly of money, but other tangibles such as a business's assets, its machinery, inventory, buildings, and real estate also constitute a portion of its capital. Classical writers such as Joseph Schumpeter, for instance, argue that only money that is available to "confront the world of goods" can be considered to be capital.[6] Labor is not considered capital because it is paid for by means of wages, and the "capital is used up."

But in the context of the value relationship, all resources that are capable of entering into and sustaining a relationship in which change and response to change are vital can be considered as capital. From our perspective, the fund also constitutes a reservoir of "goodwill." That is, it contains an article of faith in the overall functioning of the value relationship and its ability to foster growth and profitability.

Management

When we conceive of the business as participating in a value relationship, we can see that management functions divide into five areas of concentration:

1. *Customer consciousness.* Managers focus on ensuring appropriate contacts on all levels of the business so that information is direct, firsthand, fresh, and experienced in light of what the business intended for the product and its enablement.

2. *Communications.* Managers articulate the mission and reinforce the patterns of culture in ways that determine the organization's ability to respond to its value relationships. These include actions and decisions that pertain to personnel assignment and motivation and that promote the smooth interaction between departments and specialized functions within the organization.

3. *Capital use, costs, quality control, and operational effectiveness.* Capital is a limited resource, and once it is spent, it is gone. Managers ensure that resources are allocated efficiently—preventing duplication, overlapping, and waste—and effectively—putting everything to the best use. Managers must resolve conflicts and fashion compromises or solutions that allow for continued operations under whatever conditions in which the organization finds itself. Quality must be maintained on the most minute of levels, while keeping the system's overall flow intact.

4. *Continuity and innovation.* Managers ensure proper timing of resource availability and proper control of resource assignment. The pressure to act in life is related to time, and "business time" is counted off in terms of the enablement's rate of turnover. Decision makers within the organization, at whatever level they are found (and however they are vested with that role), determine the time frame for consolidating and acting on decisions and coordinating all the resources necessary in a timely way so that once a course is decided on, actions can ensue. Once this is done, managers have to make sure that efforts avoid duplication, overlap, or other wasteful intrusions.

5. *Consistency.* Once the organization establishes a value relationship with customers, no effort can be spared to sustain it. As we said, the relationship between a business and its customers is unequal. It is not that customers are hostile to the business, or that the value re-

lationship is in a battle of "us against them." It is just that people who use enablements do not hold the product itself uppermost in their hearts and minds. Their concern is what they want to accomplish with it. Despite this disheartening fact, managers must maintain the level of effort necessary to sustain the business in its environment.

Management Function Versus Management Positions. The key element of the management *function* is to keep customer requirements in the forefront of everyone's attention and to bring about conditions that ensure the organization's awareness of customer requirements, even against employees' immediate self-interest. The management function is the means by which people in the organization (1) develop a conception of the status of its essential relationships and (2) instill its discipline within the organization. If we look at management functions as actions and decisions that participate in the survival and/or success of the organization in its value relationships, we can see that to a greater or lesser extent, many people besides those in management positions have a role in decision-making responsibilities.

In most organizations, however, these management *functions* are consolidated into management *positions* that concentrate the pervasive functions into specialized viewpoints and disciplines such as finance or marketing and are then further divided into levels of authority and power. Managers adopt the standpoint of being "professional" and "objective" about the organization's value relationships with its customers. These specialists select certain factors of the organization's value relationships and reformulate them into rational measures such as sales volume, net and gross profit, market share, return on investment, and cash flow.

Professional managers undertake their specialties in the spirit of responsibility for the organization and its performance. To a greater or lesser extent, then, management disengages from immersion in the immediacy of the organization's value relationships. With the notion of responsibility, managers act with the "whole picture" in mind—the aggregate of the business's value relationships, an ideal or a model, a selective sampling—and take on the role of guardian of his or her conception of that relationship. Professional managers believe that their formulations of the relationship are accurate and provide a meaningful picture of what is actually happening in that relationship. They advocate for their means of measurement and then advocate for actions based on the conclusions drawn from those measurements.

In a business's start-up phase, management positions are not an issue. Everyone in the company is focused on making the product itself and/or establishing the business's value relationships. Either the product will be a success, and a value relationship will be formed, or else the product and its producer will disappear, without fanfare or notice. An organization needs professional management positions when the business has established value relationships with customers—when it is in a continual state of responding to them, meeting their expectations and anticipations. This situation arises when circumstances such as the following predominate in the course of a business's activities:

- When the speed of market turnover accelerates owing to technical innovation, merger activity, intervention from other national markets, and the like.
- When, owing to pace of market turnover and/or the intensity of competition, precedent is no longer a sufficient basis for determining a market response, that is, when anticipating new customer requirements becomes a dominant organizational priority.
- When the business's ability to respond requires frequent review and adjustment, affecting all levels of the business's structural and functional divisions, even its culture and mission.

Once this value relationship is established, the organization must be able to continue to respond to the demand by mustering its own initiative and marshaling its own resources. The organization must be set and ready to go. Its actions must satisfy current market conditions (not the conditions that a buyer faced the last time this action was performed) and must do it in accord with the real anticipations of the buyers (which have likewise changed since the last transaction, owing to experience with the enablement as well as competition, etc.). Setting priorities and guiding those actions constitute the purpose of the organizational component of value strategy, to which we now turn our attention.

NOTES

1. "CEO Disease," *Business Week*, April 1, 1991, p. 52.
2. Harold Geneen, *Managing* (New York: Doubleday, 1984), p. 78.
3. "Raise at ITT Raises Hackles," *Business Week*, April 29, 1991, p. 38.
4. Andrew Campbell and Kiran Tawadey, *Mission and Business Philosophy: Winning Employee Commitment* (Oxford, England: Heinemann, 1990), p. 315.
5. Edgar H. Schein, *Organizational Culture and Leadership* (San Francisco: Jossey-Bass, 1985), p. 6.
6. Joseph A. Schumpeter, *Theory of Economic Development* (Cambridge, Mass.: Harvard University Press, 1934), p. 117.

8

The Holographic Organization

It would be comforting to believe that managers could ensure success for their companies merely by reorienting and adjusting their outward-directed actions toward buyers and markets. But in business, as in personal life, maintaining a relationship is a two-way street. To be able to respond to the changing requirements of buyer demand and the world changing forces of turnover, a business has to be able to change itself. It is incumbent on an organizational strategy, therefore, to provide a framework for change and development within the business.

A business is a social unit that assembles all resources, skills, energies, and knowledge necessary and organizes them into operations that provide for the availability of a specific enablement. Accordingly, if the primary activity of business is to create value within and/or by means of a value relationship, the primary activity that creates value is also the activity that creates the organization.

The crucial determination for a business's decision makers is, What activities, projects, operations, and functions should receive priority? This determination is relatively straightforward if an organization is firmly resolved on its mission, culture, capital, and management. But when the organization must face changes in its customers' demands and market turnover, the business's organization is also disrupted. Deciding on priorities becomes more difficult, and the importance of strategy rises proportionately.

A strategy acts as a guide to help decision makers sort out which activities are more important on a daily, even momentary, basis. It helps all people involved to understand which of their many options should have priority in terms of attention, resources, and energy at any one time. A strategy channels activities toward specific, desired outcomes.

The first strategic question that arises, for instance, is, What is the goal of the business's activities—to achieve market share, to receive high quarterly returns on equity, or to please the customer? Another question that affects the outcome of determining priorities is, Who makes the decisions? A person that is given a lot of leeway in decision making might arrive at a different set of priorities than one whose actions are monitored and supervised closely.

A strategy comes into play when decision makers want only certain outcomes and not others. Strategies reflect conscious choices, and so a business's strategy for change closely reflects the conception the business has of itself—the beliefs, goals, and orientations of its owners, managers, stakeholders, or whoever else has a part in decision making.

Yet, as we all know, the hardest thing to know is oneself. For the business decision maker, this truism translates into the difficulty of perceiving just what the basis, presuppositions, and orientations of the business's decisions actually are. Strategy concerns not just customer demands or market pressures; it reflects the nature of the business itself. A strategy is never finally established or ideally shaped to all the conditions and/or exigencies it faces in the marketplace. A business is a part of a relationship; it both shapes and is shaped by participating in that relationship.

THE IMAGE OF THE BUSINESS AS A LIVING ORGANISM

In his seminal work *Images of Organization,* Gareth Morgan provides us with several images and concepts that we find useful in describing organizations.[1] We find two of these images most helpful. One is that of the organization conceived of as a living system, as an organism or as a colony of organisms, and the other is the organization conceived of as a "brain."

The image of the organization as an organism strengthens our idea that a business participates in a relationship. An organism is tightly bound to its environment and has a very specific role to play in it. If the organism is to survive, it must evolve and change over time in response to environmental circumstances. Morgan quotes Kenneth Boulding in characterizing the idea of an evolutionary process as one that promotes "the 'survival of the fitting,' not just the survival of the fittest." Morgan emphasizes that organizations in their environments, or businesses in their markets, are engaged in a process of "co-creation." He continues: "They can play an active role in shaping their future, especially when acting in concert with other organizations. Environments then become in some measure always *negotiated environments* [italics ours], rather than independent external forces."[2]

This image accords with our own idea of the business as a participant in a relationship with customers that is directly and forcefully affected by pressures of turnover. The business's mode of survival has to fit with and respond to customers' demands. In so doing, the actions it takes has an effect on its markets, creating pressures on competitors and customers alike. And, on the other hand, exactly to the degree that it cannot master or completely control everything in that environment, the business organization must also operate within the parameters of that environment. The environment is "negotiated" in that each business is acting to position itself through its interactions within its markets. As it does, it creates conditions other businesses must respond to; but since its power to affect markets is limited, it is also subject to the prevailing conditions of that market environment.

The organism image highlights the business's ability, and indeed its requirement, to change and innovate in response to environmental conditions. As Morgan says, the image "encourages us to see organizations as interacting processes that have to be balanced internally as well as in relation to the environment."[3]

For us, there is another primary advantage of using the analogy of the organization as an intelligent organism as well: Just as an organism doesn't suddenly or instantaneously "transmogrify" into a wholly new being, the business adapts to its environment while preserving some continuity with its past. Changes in organizations happen incrementally, moving from one area to another, until suddenly one realizes that the organization has evolved over time into a new shape.

In the terms of this organism analogy, the four components of the business organization we have identified can be thought of in these ways:

- The *mission* is analogous to the business's genetic code: It carries the essential messages and instructions that guide the organism's conduct in its current environment and that also serve as the blueprint for how it evolves in the face of changes in that environment.

- *Culture* comprises the relational, reactive, and emotive aspects of the business. Initially, a business's culture is the set of understandings between people within the company that permit them to interact in meaningful, purposeful, and comprehensible ways. But on a deeper level, culture comprises the qualities of energy, sensitivity, focus, and openness with which the business interacts in its environment.

- *Capital* is the capacity of the organization to make judgments about its future.

- *Management* can be considered to be a mental function of the business organization that takes in and processes information in order to respond to its environment in the form of decisions and actions.

THE HOLOGRAPHIC ORGANIZATION

The main disadvantage of the "organism" image, in Morgan's view, is that it is "far too concrete." Organizations, he says, "are very much products of visions, ideas, norms and beliefs, so that their shape and structure is much more fragile and tentative than the material structure of an organism."[4] To add proper complexity and conceptualization to this image of organization, he offers the image of the organization as a brain.

By this image he does not mean only that an organization is an entity that merely processes information. Contemporary images conceive of the brain as a "holographic" system in which each part of the system replicates the whole; or, we might say, the whole system—the whole brainlike organization—is "enfolded" or contained in each part or member of the system. As a result, if the image is broken, any single piece can reconstruct the whole, albeit with a loss in detail and definition.[5]

In terms of strategy, this image has meaning because it points to the importance each member of the business has in terms of creating a dynamic and successful organization. Value strategy regards each member of the organization as contributing something that allows the organization to act responsively, energetically, and appropriately to its value relationships. In this light, the more an individual assumes personal responsibility for the organization's mission, the more freedom and discretion the organization will have in carrying out its mission. The more people are not fully involved in taking responsibility for the mission, however, the easier it is for an organization to lose its focus and concentration with each change and response it must undertake.

As Morgan points out, the whole organization defines itself and creates itself, or recreates itself, in response to environmental demands. "Get the whole into the parts; create connectivity and redundancy; create simultaneous specialization and generalization; create a capacity to self-organize: these are the things that have to be done to create holographic organization," says Morgan.[6] The organization will succeed or fail depending on how well the whole is accepted by the parts and how well the parts can adapt, change responsibilities, or create new ones while still having the organization's mission in mind. This is the essence of the strategic importance of holographic organizational design.

Morgan cites four "interacting principles" that enable organizations to achieve a holographic design:

1. *Redundant functions.* The whole is built into the parts by having a combination of specialization and generalization built into each position, operation, and function in the organization. "Instead of spare parts being added to a system," that is, added positions filled with people who have sole proprietorship of a function or knowledge, "extra functions are added to each of the operating parts so that each part is able to engage in a range of functions rather than just perform a single specialized activity."[7]

2. *Requisite variety.* The complexity and variety of a person's job and working environment match the challenges posed by its external environment: "All the elements of an organization should embody critical dimensions of the environment with which they have to deal, so that they can self-organize to cope with the demands they are likely to face."[8]

3. *Minimum critical specification.* This principle allows members of the organization to apply the previous two principles in ways that are most appropriate for the situation as it affects their function and role within the organization.

4. *Learning to learn.* This principle recognizes and encourages the ability of each member of the organization to change and adapt to changes in the environment with creativity and commitment to the organization's well-being.

Another way of expressing the principles of holographic organization is that of encouraging what Robert A. Burgelman calls "autonomous strategic behavior" in each of the business's members.[9] The organization's strategy is accepted by everyone as a communal enterprise. Everyone in the organization is recognized for their "opportunity-seeking behavior,"[10] and from this recognition come ideas for meaningful organizational responses to the environment. In terms of our hologram analogy, if some members of the organization do not contribute or do not fulfill their roles, breaking off pieces of the photographic plate, so to speak, the organization's efforts lose sharpness, clarity, and effectiveness.

The "Quantum Brain" Analogy

In Morgan's "brain" image, information is processed with a view toward creating and recreating the entire organization. Another image that augments and supports Morgan's is provided by physicist and theorist Roger Penrose. In his book *The Emperor's New Mind*, he makes the distinction between thinking of the brain as a mechanistic computer that processes information by means of set "algorithms" or formulas and

82

THE BUSINESS

thinking of the brain as a "quantum computer."[11] Whereas the former model assumes that the brain operates according to a rigid, "natural," and virtually unalterable pattern, the quantum model assumes the opposite. It envisions the brain as an evolving entity that actually changes itself, adapts itself to the world it has created while taking in new information.

In Penrose's conception, the brain has the capacity to create new algorithms and patterns for understanding and surviving in the environment. By analogy, the organization so conceived has the ability to use information, concepts, strategies, technologies, and resources to change itself and augment its ability to perform in its changing environment. Or, as Morgan says, "New capacities will lead to new organizational forms."[12]

Eventually, in a kind of "quantum leap," the accumulation of new functions and actions actually creates a whole new level of awareness— the business's own "Aha"—and in the context of a value strategy, a business's quantum leap can lead to new missions and cultures and new managers—analogous to added mental capabilities and the evolution of the body form.

Conceiving of an organization as a self-contained, self-adapting, intelligent organism, all the parts of the organization can be seen as learning new functions and actions. These metaphors and images provide ideas we can draw on to develop a new conception of strategy. We can see that the role of the strategy makers is to maintain the proper focus on the source of change in the environment and to foster this process throughout the organization. Strategy is an outlook on change that each person adopts and implements.

Thus, the strategy itself is distributed. On the "cellular" or individual member level, that strategy is translated so as to pertain to the precise situation that person is facing. The organization is not contained within a structure into which people have to fit and contend. Rather, the organization *is* the strategy that each person carries around in his or her head, heart, and hand in order to meet the day's new challenges.

The Strategic Decision Makers

Of course, an organization changes because someone or some group of people decide to make changes. So, we must ask, who initiates this organizational strategy? Who is it that defines the strategic guidelines we have alluded to for each component of the organization? A typical answer is that these organizational concerns are the province of the "upper" management "chiefs"—CEOs, CFOs, and COOs— and/or officers. A familiar plaint in the strategic consulting world is that change is something ordered from the top to be carried out by the middle on the bottom. And, to be sure, people in so-called top positions must be involved to ensure that the changes do occur, are reviewed, modified, and carried forward once again. But we must say, people in these positions are not the sole conceivers and implementors of organizational change.

In fact, in terms of our analogy, just as each cell adapts in order to keep functioning within a changing environment, so each member of the organization participates in strategic organizational change. Each member of the organization takes part in and contributes in some measure to these organizational components. The factors that limit this participation are either organizational constraints that stifle this kind of participation or an individual's own lack of motivation.

HOLOGRAPHIC ORGANIZATION AND VALUE STRATEGY

The purpose of the organizational component of value strategy is to keep the organization focused on the source of the changes in its environment—customer demands and markets—and to keep the business organization in an appropriate state of readiness for appropriate internal change and adaptation. Strategy promotes appropriate organizational changes while supporting the continuity of decision making and practices that give the business its identity.

We have taken time to develop this idea because this conception of the organization has several important implications for developing an organizational strategy.

1. A business organization is a participant in a living relationship with its customers and its markets. So we can rightly think of the business as having a life of its own.

2. Although it is subject to the forces unleashed by the actions of others, it is still a self-defining entity, capable of change and capable of exerting its own influence within its domain and markets.

3. The organization is affected as a whole by what occurs in the course of its life. Each member, not just an insulated core of top managers, forms part of the organism.

4. Decisions on the course and effectiveness of the business's relationships and its life in its environment are made every day, each moment, by all its members, and they use their own conception of what that business is about in order to make those decisions.

5. A business's action is not primarily directed at its output but at its capacity to remain a functioning and living entity. Its output is important: It is the basis for the business's existence, and it is the

end result of its process and activity. But if either the business or the output had to go, it is clear what decision would have to be made.

6. The organization acts as a "filter" of its own reality. By that we mean a business's organization—how people are put into relation to one another—selects the information, impressions, and readings of the world that an organization is able and willing to process and deal with. As Andrew Van de Ven says, the organization "serves to sort attention," channeling attention to some aspects of a situation in one direction and other aspects of it in other directions.[13] This sorting out determines how the business responds in the context of its value relationship, that is, what the business actually produces.

The particular form of organization a business assumes reflects the way it conceives its essential value relationship, and the extent to which the business internalizes those relationships and makes them its own. Value strategy seeks out the source of change, which for us is the essential fact that people will want to buy the products and services businesses produce. Change is a direct outcome of the fact that people are receptive to new products and business is amply capable of supplying what their (or another business's) customers envision. Thus, a business's success or survival is not dependent on market share or return on equity; these are only derivative results of the primary accomplishment—that of maintaining a value relationship with those customers.

Value strategy assigns highest priority to those business actions that have creating value at stake or as their goal. Some activities are more focused on creating value than others. For example, dealing with governmental paperwork is necessary, mandated by law, and required because it contributes to the overall social conditions that make doing business possible. But it does not contribute directly to creating value; so it will have a low priority in the hierarchy of strategic considerations. Ordering equipment necessary for production does contribute directly to the business's ability to create value and so should command a high priority in the minds of decision makers.

When adopting a value strategy, a business must be able to affect its very own core. For a business to be able to respond to changes in buyer requirements and market pressures, it must be able to change itself. Thus, we have to look at the core experiences, concepts, and precepts of business practice, and these *must* be open to change.

NOTES

1. Gareth Morgan, *Images of Organization* (Newbury Park, Calif.: Sage, 1986).
2. Ibid., pp. 69–70.

3. Ibid., p. 72.

4. Ibid., p. 74.

5. Ibid., p. 80.

6. Ibid., pp. 97–98.

7. Ibid., p. 99.

8. Ibid., p. 100.

9. Robert A. Burgelman, "Corporate Entrepreneurship and Strategic Management: Insights from a Process Study," *Management Science* 29, no. 12 (December 1983): 1355.

10. Ibid., p. 1354.

11. Roger Penrose, *The Emperor's New Mind: Concerning Computers, Minds and the Laws of Physics* (New York: Oxford University Press, 1989).

12. Morgan, *Images of Organization*, p. 91.

13. Andrew H. Van de Ven, "Central Problems in the Management of Innovation," *Management Science* 32, no. 5 (May 1986): 596.

9

Classical Organization Strategies

In this chapter, we will look at organization strategies that use the classical assumptions about the goals of business and its essential relationships. A *capital-based strategy* strictly focuses on the rate of return on investment (ROI), or price per share of stock, as its goal and as the motivation that focuses all its relationships. A *management-based strategy* also has a goal of increasing return on investment, but it accomplishes its goals of increasing ROI by commanding market share or by optimizing rate of return within its market niche.

These strategies have their place in the contemporary business scene, since they focus on specific factors that are important for decision makers to consider. However, since they do not encourage the holographic organizational components we presented in the last chapter, they fall short of being able to adapt and evolve in response to their environments.

For one thing, they do not distribute the strategy for change and adaptation to the company's value relationships throughout the organization. These classical strategies concentrate the strategic, conceptual functions of the organization—including information processing and evaluation as well as its judgmental capabilities—into the "enclaves" of upper management. This prohibits redundancy or distribution of decision-making functions, which is the core feature of holographic organizations. Structure and culture are imposed on the employees, or the employees are "induced"[1] to ascribe to them. This also leads to a deficit in requisite variety in the work lives of the organization's members.

These organizational strategies short-circuit the kind of holographic distribution of insight, initiative, and will that it takes to meet changing buyer requirements and market turnover. They permit "tinkering" with organizational change and innovation but shy away from any significant realignment of resources or structure. We show that organizational rigidity and paralysis in the face of volatile customer demand and turnover is not a consequence of a single CEO's personality or a company's culture. It stems directly from what the company sees as its primary goal, what it exists to accomplish and for whom, how it conceives of its mission, and what relationships are essential for achieving that goal.

CAPITAL-BASED ORGANIZATION STRATEGY

Capital-based organization strategies are formulated by a single "capital strategist" or a closely knit group of allied associates. They drive the organization's resources to increase capital by aggressively increasing its rate of return on investment. Certainly this focus is necessary in a business organization. Profitability, and an appropriate return on investment, is like breathing: The business cannot survive without it. But when this orientation is taken to be the primary or only purpose of a business, impassable barriers arise in terms of organizational flexibility and responsiveness in the face of changing customer requirements and turnover.

Mission

The capital strategist is not doing business because he has to earn a living. The capital strategist freely chooses to take responsibility for the fate of a business or corporation or portfolio of businesses and investments. The capital strategist acts on the basis of what he *believes*. How much of his information, knowledge, and prior experience are applied to the decision is a matter of style. Intuition is sometimes regarded as a more reliable basis for decisions than the methods used by "scientific" management to comprehend the business and its environment. Harold Geneen typifies this approach in *Managing*: "The relationship among the numbers was for me like reading between the lines of a book.... In my mind's eye, I could see the men writing the reports I read. I got a sense of the general health of the company, the performers and non-performers, the problem areas."[2]

The mission for the capital strategist is to *have capital*. If he has capital, the capital strategist can make decisions and act. If he doesn't, he is out of the game. So his ultimate mission is to preserve this ability to act as a capital strategist. This mission may, and in fact frequently does, put the capital strategist in opposition to what a company's line managers believe to be in the best interest of the company. But this is no concern for him. In this role, the capital strategist exerts the sheer power that comes from having capital.

Nowhere in this conception of the mission is there a mention of customers, their relationship to products and to the companies that make them, or is there any mention of operations employees. The capital strategist sees himself as being aloof from the business's day-to-day value relationships. A business is seen as a collection of assets in varying states of being able to yield a return on those assets. The driving force of capital-based strategy is very much as Geneen describes it: bottom-line–driven numbers that meet the prescribed goal, no matter what. As Geneen put it, "It was the 'end' to which all my efforts at ITT would be directed, an 'end' to which I would commit myself without reservation."[3]

Culture of Organizations in Capital-Based Strategies

This kind of strategy entails operations that are confined and controlled within a very rigid structure and hierarchy. It demands that operations be deployed to consistently maximize utilization of capital (machinery and labor), wringing out every last morsel of profit and productivity. Since gains in productivity are a major source for profit, this strategy drives toward production efficiencies, to save time and money and to increase margins. Labor is regarded as a variable cost that must, above all, be kept as low as possible and is always under pressure to prove itself against encroaching automation.

In terms of how these organizations interact with their external environments and customers, only one cultural component of the three "M's" applies, that of measurement. Means are not an issue—whatever it takes to achieve the bottom line is fair game. Neither is malleability. The ability to routinely achieve results—in Geneen's case, that of 10 percent increase of ROI—is the standard. To achieve the bottom line, measurement is placed at a premium.

The capital strategist applies the most basic and rudimentary forms of measurement to a business's value relationships and eliminates from consideration all sensitivity to the actual experiences, transactions, and interactions involved with the product. Geneen expressed this commitment to strictly quantified reckoning in the form of his demand for "unshakable facts." In essence, these facts constitute a distillation of perceptions of a situation, gathered from various sources, their apparent "biases" stripped away in order to get at a "true picture," that is, one based on quantitative measurement alone.[4] In this quote from Geneen's book, it is interesting to note just what those "biases" are.

Salesmen will always reflect what their customers are telling them and *they tend to exaggerate the parameters either on the up or on the down side*; marketing men put their faith in statistical analyses of what the market should be for your product, *with little regard for what your customers are saying*; engineers usually have an idea for a new product (*which may or may not be what the market or the customers want at that time*); someone else will have a *dream* of what could happen if only . . . and someone else will have a *nightmare* about all the things that could go wrong. [Emphasis added][5]

   The biases, in other words, are different people's opinions, observations, and feelings about the nature and status of the business's value relationships. The capital strategist wants these feelings stripped away so that the "objective" criteria—as determined only by the prescribed norms and standards—can be defended. This is the same reasoning as that behind Geneen's dictum of no long-range planning. Since long-range planning must be based, in large part, on observation of or intuition about actual customer experiences with the company's products, it is taboo in this sort of capital-based strategy.[6]

   In terms of its internal culture, all the four "W's"—walls, words, wages, and will—are unidirectional: from the top down. While Geneen paid his executives 10 percent above the prevailing salary level, these wages were paid in expectation of long hours at the expense of all other aspects of the executive's life. Geneen made the final judgment as to the amount and quality of contribution the executive made to the bottom line. The cultural component of "will" was only Geneen's will.

   The "unshakable facts" were presented in the form of reports at monthly meetings of all the company's general managers that normally ran from ten in the morning to ten at night (and until midnight in Europe). Problems were "red flagged" at the top of the report. Managers were to produce reports with "crisp thinking," stripped of any "indefinite" statements. "In the future this kind of 'indefinite' statement and report will be subject to review with the author, and action will be taken on this point alone," Geneen commanded.[7]

   At these meetings, more than two hundred people read and "critiqued" the reports. No matter how sincerely Geneen believes that these meetings were models of "open communications," the reports were reviewed only within the context of Geneen's absolute authority, where the dictated standards were not to be contested. While I have no intention of impugning Geneen's good and honorable intentions, or even the wisdom of his approach, given the job he was hired to do, the unshakable fact for us remains that each manager was put in the position of seeking approval or at least the avoidance of castigation and embarrassment.

   It is important to realize that we do not intend to criticize Geneen personally. And neither do we cite his approach as being a matter of a personal management style that we happen not to like. We cite Geneen's method here, accepting its strengths as well as its weaknesses, because it is a reasonable and logical procedure that follows from the tenets, beliefs, and demands of bottom-line–focused, capital-based strategy.

Other Capital-Based Strategies

We have used the writings of Harold Geneen to describe some of the most salient features of one kind of capital-based strategy. His writings describe the variety of capital-based strategy that increases capital by the *acquisition* of assets. There is another kind of capital-based strategy that increases capital by *divesting* assets. This strategy was exerted with greatly disruptive force throughout the eighties by the investment bankers and Wall Street exponents of leveraged buyouts (LBOs). The LBO artist sells off pieces of the business on the theory that the pieces of a business are worth more as separate entities than they are when grouped together as a single business.

The typical LBO converts equity into debt, the purchasers (the managers of the company) pulling out the equity of the business's assets in the form of cash advanced by banks. When all the "fat" is stripped away—peripheral businesses are sold off and operations of the remaining business pared down to operational bare bones—the business can again go public, making new killings for the raiding owners.

In its roundup of LBOs in the eighties, *Business Week* noted that before the eighties ended, "a towering $1.3 trillion was spent on shuffling assets—an amount on a par with the annual economic output of West Germany."[8] There were 11 such deals (totaling less than $5 billion) in 1980, and 275 in 1989 (totaling nearly $58 billion).

As poignantly described by the late Max Holland in *When the Machine Stopped*,[9] the debt burden left in the wake of an LBO requires that the business maximize cash flow (to pay interest and principle): Prices are raised to the maximum; research and development (R&D) is curtailed; high-priced (often highly experienced) labor is disposed of; and payments to vendors are delayed to the latest possible moment.

"The classsical LBO took on $9 of debt for every $1 of equity," continues the *Business Week* survey.

Management typically got a 10% to 20% stake. According to calculations by Harvard University economist Michael C. Jensen, for every $1,000 increase in shareholder wealth in LBO's, top managers enjoyed an increase of $64 in personal wealth. By contrast, the chief executives of publicly held corporations, with minuscule equity stakes in their own companies, increased their wealth an average of only $3.25 for each $1,000 in shareholder wealth.[10]

The justification for this behavior is that it supposedly makes managers more "efficient" by demanding the maximal utilization of capital. Seen through the eyes of a business's value relationships, that rationale can be translated this way: It subjects the business as a whole to a goal that suits the capital strategist—increasing a business's yield for himself and his closed circle of investors. What it does in today's business world, however, is drain equity (including customer goodwill, vendor confidence, experienced labor capital) that is urgently needed for change and innovation in the face of turnover.

Warren Buffet, widely recognized in financial circles as the nation's most successful investor, assessed the LBO binge of the eighties this way: "The handiwork of the Wall Street of the 1980's is even worse than we had thought. Many important businesses have been mortally wounded."[11]

Still, it must be pointed out that the raiders' divestment strategy is successful only because the capital strategists on the *inside* of a corporation tacitly or explicitly allow them in or invite them in to work their "magic." The largest LBO ever conducted, the buyout of RJR Nabisco, was not initiated by either Kohlberg, Kravis and Roberts (KKR), or Shearson-Lehman American Express. It began because the capital-minded CEO of RJR Nabisco, Ross Johnson, was determined to find a way to increase the value of the company's stock. In the end, he lost control of the company but netted a $53 million "golden parachute" payoff. His number two, Ed Horigan, took home $45.7 million.[12]

The Barriers Created by Capital-Based Strategy

Capital-based strategies erect barriers to organizational change by channeling all the organization's resources, energy, and intelligence toward one, and only one, goal. The decisions of the organization are made in a relational vacuum, giving credence only to abstract data, stripped of all human content—whether that content is in the form of ambiguity, opportunity, or speculation. This one goal of ROI is elevated to a position of prominence that excludes other organizational goals from consideration.

The capital strategist doesn't deal with a business's value relationships per se but only with some of its effects and results, the numbers on the balance sheet or "facts," with the ambiguities of actual value relationships with customers distilled out.

In many cases, the local efforts of the single business's decision makers are outweighed by general socioeconomic considerations that are of importance to the capital strategist. Since capital is measured by the amount of money accumulated as a return on investment, the growth or diminution of capital is as much determined by generalized monetary and economic factors as it is by the particular success of any specific investment. Thus, no matter how wise a particular investment may be from the standpoint of a business's value relationships, factors such as international monetary fluctuations, general social inflation, and recession in industries, regions, or whole nations act as prime determinants for decisions.

Capital-based organization strategies may work, and they did work when markets were stable and broad based over long periods of time. Then businesses had the opportunity to develop economies of scale, to increase productivity through the introduction of new machines or organizational efficiencies. Turnover, however, creates conditions in which capital is dearly needed for rapid, and often costly, innovation. In the end, capital-based organizational strategies squander capital.

Capital-based strategies squander capital in a business climate that is marked by changing customer demands and turnover because they focus on acquiring or divesting assets that are at some point on the upper part of their cycle in relationships with customers. What is seen by the capital strategist is only the price-to-earnings (P/E) ratio, meaning that the business's value relationships have already been established and are producing income for its investors. Capital-based strategies wring that value out of the relationship. They use capital to obtain an immediate "return," not to develop and augment those relationships for the long term or to plan and institute changes in the organization that can sustain the responsiveness such a relationship requires.

MANAGEMENT-BASED ORGANIZATION STRATEGY

The second type of classical strategy we will discuss is management-based organization strategy—a kind of strategy devised and implemented by managers who have full operational control of the company. Capital is supplied out of operating profits and/or by shareholders. Management strategy is a variant of capital-based strategy in that the standard for performance is still to increase return on investment and achieve an aggressive rate of growth. However, management-based strategy differs from capital-based strategy in one important respect: Management-based strategy is directed at *markets* rather than at the assets and/or equity of the companies themselves.

This form of organization strategy took shape in the United States at the beginning of the century, under the guiding hand of organizational geniuses such as Pierre du Pont, and was perfected by Alfred P. Sloan. It reached its zenith of influence in the sixties. As business scholars Alfred Chandler and Peter Drucker are quick to point out, these innovators gave shape to organizational strategies emulated and employed as models—until recently, that is—throughout the Western, non-Communist world.

Chandler points out that the modern corporation had its roots in imitating military organizational models that collected, standardized, and directed the energies of many specialties within a single organization to serve growing numbers of people spread out over the vast U.S. land-scape.[13] By means of acquisitions, enterprising decision makers vertically integrated their companies, incorporating all the specialized functions necessary to make a product and get it to the market. Since businesses accumulated special operations that replicated or reflected the demands of their particular markets, determining an organization's "structure" was tantamount to making its strategy.

Under this umbrella of corporate strategy, managers evolved as a new class of specialized practitioners. With the strategy/structure in place, they concentrated on getting the numbers straight, organizing their respective disciplines into logical and quantifiable procedures that could promise predictable results. They oversaw these specialized functions and reported on the firm's performance to its holders of capital.

Pierre du Pont added an all-important strategic innovation. He demonstrated how the notion of "market share" could be used as a means to ensure steady growth and profitability, even through economic downturns. The aim of Du Pont's strategy was not to achieve a monopoly in a market (which a capital strategist might think desirable) but to command a significant market share. Controlling a commanding market share enables the company to influence prices in the markets and also allows for sufficient economies of scale to keep prices both low and profitable. When a downturn occurs, this price advantage protects its status as a supplier of choice.

Organizations thus became attuned to the nuances of economic and competitive forces operating in those markets. This insight paved the way for the "science of management," which used specialized market data and economic analysis to make decisions and formulate strategy based on price, differentiation, market share, and refinements of economies of scale.

By the early fifties, Alfred P. Sloan saw the need to refine the pillars of management strategy. By establishing subdivisions within the firm, strategy was able to address the needs of more focused market segments. The structure of the firm thus reflected the growing purchasing power of the American public and their growing diversification of needs.

The ranks of managers were further diversified into "corporate" managers, who devised strategy and oversaw the performance of the whole organization, and "line" managers, who directed their energies toward their respective market segments. The corporate managers employed the quantitative methods of capital strategists and emulated their detached approach. Overseeing each particular business's performance was left to the care of the line managers. Sloan thus seemed to achieve the best of both worlds. He imported the analytical acumen of the capital strategist while paying increased attention to what the market demanded.

Mission

The key insight of management-based strategy is that so many products can now be made available to such diverse populations, distinguished by education, income, geographical location, and other factors, that its markets must be *influenced* by how a business presents and supports its products.

To do this, management strategies attempt to control their market segments. Managers believe that they know what products the consumer will buy, presumably, because their company produces them; managers also know what kind of system is necessary to produce this product. The organization is thus regarded as a "machine," a tool, the levers of which are information, labor, matériel, capital, vendors, and distributors.

Managers use techniques over which they have control and authority to affect that performance. These techniques utilize advertising, price manipulation, political and material leverage, and other classical competitive strategies to influence and protect market share. The manager's work is to leverage the organization's existing assets and strengths to their fullest extent in order to achieve those effects.

So while products are regarded as meeting needs that are influenced by market changes, style, and the press of competition, the product itself is less at stake for management than utilizing the assets in place to maximize profits or return on the investment. Product decisions are made (as much as possible) conservatively, that is, within "known" market parameters, in order to fully utilize the company's assets on the scale at which production efficiencies can be achieved. As many aspects of the product as possible are shaped and determined by investments already amortized; the quality of the products and performance features are as much tailored to meet the company's internal requirements as they are focused on the quality and the performance of the product as perceived by customers.

Thus, the mission of management-based strategy is divided: Its goal and the means of attaining that goal are not necessarily on the same track. On the one hand, markets and buyers are calling for major changes in a product; using cars as an example, pollution controls and higher gas efficiency are mandated by government, whereas buyers want improved quality and new engineering features such as antilock brakes and air bags. But spending capital to meet these demands goes against the capital strategist's requirement of achieving profitability from quarter to quarter.

IBM chairman John F. Akers articulated this divided focus perfectly in a cautionary memorandum to his employees. In this memorandum, he was bemoaning IBM's loss of market share and its inability to bring out successful products in a timely fashion. "I.B.M. exists to provide a return to its shareholders. We do that by creating satisfied and delighted customers—more of them than our competitors," he said.[14]

True to form, the divided mission often means that people in different parts of the organization are frequently working at crossed purposes. Line managers, still in close proximity to markets, may want to make changes in products. But since these changes may affect the structure and strategies devised by the corporate brain trust, which has maximizing returns as its goal, and since these are the people who pass judgment on promotions and career advancement, the changes either are whittled down to fit the demands of capital or are not even recommended.

The higher up the corporate ladder, the more managers adopt the capital-based goal to increase ROI. Organizational change and product innovation are both locked out until such a time as the effect of the paralysis shows in the reports of the bottom line: market share lost, sales down, profits shrinking.

Culture

Management functions become directly identified with management positions. Managers secure and defend their monopoly on the business's strategy, measurement, and organizational prerogatives as dictated, formulated, and reported in the highly specialized language of their particular discipline. Each position reflects how its slant or point of view on the business's situation is able to frame problems and solutions in the most appropriate manner, thus occupying a driving position of power in the organization as a whole. Workers down the line perform routine, repetitive, narrowly focused tasks that are prescribed in all regards by management's decisions and are closely monitored and measured from on high.

Rather than rely on interaction among its members for initiating changes, management-based strategies depend on two types of "energizing" influences in their ranks: leaders and expertise.

Leaders, who set out directions (point to where the "goalposts are," as Geneen would say), are prized by classically oriented organizations because they move management beyond their self-defined parameters of success, open up new visions of what constitutes its markets. *Expertise* translates a general situation, problem, or process into the specific terms of a single discipline or group of disciplines. Their solutions fit classical organizational strategies because they can be digested easily within the business's segmented disciplines, departments, and rubrics.

As we shall see in a later chapter, the literature of classical management science preaches about how a business cannot do without leaders and experts. Experts and leaders reach beyond the strictures of routine, the high walls and constricted words and will of the organization's culture. But in practice, managers are highly ambivalent about the presence of these people in their midst, and they are judged to be a mixed blessing at best. Executives find these types difficult to deal with and often find that they are not able to integrate into the organization's culture.

Experts expend a great deal of time and energy promoting the efficacy of a particular perspective and way of doing things. They have "won" when their particular variation of method that the expertise makes possible can institute, implement, and validate the performance of the management-based strategy. Thus, companies become known as "marketing driven" or "bottom-line driven" or "technology driven." They are often subject to the "priority of the week," depending on which expert has the ear of the key decision maker. Leaders, however, are iconoclasts, loners, and rebels.[15]

As a result, both types are as likely to be drummed out of the organization as they are to have their talents, insights, and energies used by its established managers. Quite often, their insights and ideas are commercially viable; and indeed, the story of many a Silicon Valley enterprise is one of how its founder was working for a company that wouldn't buy into his ideas, so he started his own company.

The Intractable Contradictions of Management-Based Strategy

Since the management-based strategy is focused on markets, and so is closer in its orientation to a business's core value relationships, it does seem to offer a more viable and robust basis for strategy. But whatever advantage it gains by virtue of its attention to markets, it loses because it divides its energies.

Management-based organization strategy is split in two different directions. Even though it focuses its attention on the business's relationship to its markets, the intent of this focus is not to serve those markets but to exploit them for another purpose: to increase capital and ROI. Thus, management uses markets as its stage, platform, or arena in which it *performs* for capital.

The criteria for judging the performance of management are measured against some rubric that tracks results in absolute terms. Performance against these standards is measured by an amalgam of "objective," quantified gauges and ratios: the performance of all the company's operations as a whole, profits and growth as expressed by measures such as gross and net profit, ROI, cash flow, and market share. But all these measures are merely different ways to assess the status and trends of that key and single measure, ROI.

As a result, management-based strategy ends up facing three unresolvable contradictions.

1. *Information*. The first contradiction pertains to a manager's primary function within the organization—that of being the clearinghouse for information gathering, processing, interpretation, and dissemination. Managers apply scientific methods—quantification, statistical analysis, trend mapping—in order to guide the organization into the future. They do this by breaking the events and happenings observed in the organization's value relationships into disciplines; data are gathered, collated, quantified, and analyzed into coherent marketing reports, cash flow analyses, productivity ratios, and the like.

The information only comes together when a decision is to be made at the top of the organization. The decision and some selected supporting facts are disseminated back down through the ranks and out to the customer in the form of products and services.

Each of these disciplines relates to customers through the hierarchic channels of the management funnel. Thus, managers channel most of their creative energies and benefits from their knowledge to the top of the pyramid, to the people who are responsible for their promotions and raises.

And herein lies the contradiction.

The management function is necessary only because this kind of information—gathered, organized, and made meaningful according to some standard—is the necessary and irreducible basis for a business to act effectively in its markets and respond to its value relationships. The role of management is to use information to instill in the organization a readiness and ability to respond appropriately on the basis of that information.

And yet management is less able to use this information in order to effect changes and consolidate ideas for innovation and response because its reporting structure and line of authority and accountability are only directed upward, toward the capital decision makers that are most removed from the company's value relationships.

Since upper management's goal is linked to that of capital, financial control and administration take on prominent roles in allocating and organizing resources. Their demands even take precedence over those value-based activities for which line managers have responsibility, such as product development, familiarity with buyers and their requirements, and sacrificial level of investment. Thus, the usefulness and efficacy of the line manager's information often break down by the time the information moves in the downward direction, toward the people on the production line. The result is organizational paralysis in the face of change.

2. *Responsiveness and innovation.* The second contradiction has to do with the manager's ability to respond to market changes. Assuming the manager's actions have been successful, these same actions will precipitate the necessity for new ventures. As Peter Drucker says, "Success always obsoletes the very behavior that achieved it. It always creates new realities. It always creates, above all, its own and different problems."[16] The manager always must face the new venture. Since change and future orientation constitute the raison d'être of management, it would seem that change presents no particular difficulty to management.

However, since in classical strategies a manager's performance is evaluated according to the capital-based goal of ROI and market share, each time the new venture—indeed, the need for a new venture—disrupts the supposed predictable success of the status quo. To suggest change therefore puts the manager's position—his authority, status, and power—at risk.

To even raise these questions puts the status quo at risk. The manager ultimately has to go out of the bounds of packaged information and comfortable assumptions. He has to leave behind the formulas and equations that had once made sense of his world and has to venture out once again to view the product in the milieu of its transactions. From this information, new assessments of the reality of the new value process must be developed. Then standards and practices of the organization must be matched to this new reality. A new value relationship must be constituted by decisive actions.

Since managers' career advancement depends on the measurement of their performance, they become invested in their interpretations of the business's value relationship. They become *defensive.* The perception of risk increases when the organization is viewed within the classical outlook that it must perform according to certain "universal" standards, must achieve certain concrete results, and must submit to its own declared rational and scientific criteria for evaluation. These defensive managerial controls diminish and reduce which options for action will be deemed "feasible," rather than expand and enhance the choices that are available.

3. *Organizational change.* Finally, management positions contradict their primary role of managing and fostering organizational change. Since creating change is not done at a distance, management must change itself—or it is replaced. There is no choice. The organization lives or dies with its ability to change with regard to the reality of the value relation; and within that organization, management itself will live or die according to the status of the business within its domain of effective value relations. Managers create either organizational limits or oppor-

tunities. They are either capable and willing to undertake organizational change in accordance with the terms of its essential value relationship or that relationship slips out of its grasp, leaving the empty husks of management's objectified terms, standards, and conditions.

When changes do impinge on the organization, politics enters the scene; people become defensive and protective of their "turf." As a result, only small changes occur. Individual managers strive to preserve their own position by whittling down the potential opened up by opportunities in the business's value relationships.

The hierarchical structure and upward-directed line of authority in classical organizations do serve the ostensibly useful purpose of insulating lower echelons of line managers and workers from change-induced turmoil. These structures create the appearance of a smooth, orderly, and rational production process. But that is far from the truth. In the rarified air of the corporate executive suites, political battles often rage on like vicious Olympian wars among the gods. Some people achieve great victories, while others are banished.

In addition to the pain to individuals caused by this kind of behavior, something much more destructive is going on: Even though the battle that rages above may occur out of sight to most people in the organization, its effects take the form of decisions not being made, opportunities not being taken up, and morale slipping. The organization languishes as markets and competitors move on.

NOTES

1. Robert A. Burgelman, "Corporate Entrepreneurship and Strategic Management: Insights from a Process Study," *Management Science* 29, no. 12 (December 1983): 1350.

2. Harold Geneen, *Managing* (New York: Doubleday, 1984), p. 37.

3. Ibid., p. 41.

4. Ibid., pp. 115–117.

5. Ibid., pp. 116–117.

6. Ibid., p. 88.

7. Ibid., p. 95.

8. "The Best Deals of the 1980's," *Business Week*, January 15, 1990, p. 52.

9. Max Holland, *When the Machine Stopped: A Cautionary Tale from American Industry* (Boston: Harvard Business School Press, 1989).

10. "The Best and Worst Deals of the 1980's," *Business Week*, January 15, 1990, p. 58.

11. "The Bullish and Bearish Moves by Buffett," *New York Times*, May 6, 1991, p. D10.

12. Bryan Burrough and John Helyar, *Barbarians at the Gate: The Fall of RJR Nabisco* (New York: Harper & Row, 1990), pp. 506–507.

13. Alfred D. Chandler, *The Visible Hand: The Managerial Revolution in American Business* (Cambridge, Mass.: Belknap Press, 1977).

14. "IBM's Chief Criticizes Staff Again."*New York Times*, June 19, 1991, p. D5.

15. Abraham Zaleznik, "Managers and Leaders, Are They Different?" in *Strategic Management, Harvard Business Review Executive Book Series*, Richard G. Hamermesh, ed. (New York: John Wiley, 1983), p. 454.

16. Peter F. Drucker, *Management: Tasks, Responsibilities, Practices* (New York: Harper & Row, 1974), p. 88.

10

The Value Organization Strategy

Value strategy is "customer focused." Decision makers bring customers' concerns into the business's daily life either by emulating or by closely empathizing with their requirements. The intent of a value-based strategy is to maximize the use of the company's resources in the face of change and to enable it to respond with a companywide commitment to those changes.

Managers do not choose to adopt a value strategy. They face up to adopting one when they feel the brunt of changes in their essential value relationships—when new products appear that reshape the enablements they support; when new competitors appear that fragment markets further, creating micromarkets; when environmental concerns or new scientific evidence forces a product to be reconfigured; when turnover is accepted as a fact of life: New alliances and partnerships change the nature of a market's integration. Then a value strategy becomes a matter of survival, and the real work of business decision making begins.

As insightful writers on the subject—Rosabeth Moss Kantor, Andrew Van de Ven, Gareth Morgan, and Robert Burgelman, to name a few—are quick to point out, product innovation and organizational innovation go hand in hand. When responding to customer demand and volatile markets, product innovations that incorporate truly new ideas often require new organizational structures and practices. Organizations with strict hierarchy and highly segmented departments encourage "tinkering," as Van de Ven says, but not innovation.[1] Departmentalized hierarchies constrict both the information necessary to trigger change and the resources that can be applied to change within protected enclaves of status, authority, and self-validating methodologies.

In the face of changing customer requirements, value strategy strives to guide the organization toward maintaining the atmosphere, resources, and commitment for innovation, both in terms of product and service innovations and in terms of organizational innovation. But this is no easy task. Organizational change in the face of changing environmental requirements is tantamount to self-guided organizational evolution. It is an attempt to change the organism's makeup while it is in the midst of trying to survive. In this light, we can see the importance of the holographic image of the organization we have been using. The intent of this image is to provide for the intellectual, experiential, and information-processing mechanisms necessary to undertake organizational evolution.

Organizational change thus has a distinctive status in value strategy. In the classical models, strategy is more or less reflected in the "organizational chart," which lays out the lines of authority in the chain of command. It is a static model. In contrast, value strategy defines the organization dynamically, in terms of the actions it must carry out in its markets and the relationships it maintains with its customers.

We can see an example of this kind of value-based organizational thinking in the preamble to Hewlett-Packard's "Statement of Corporate Objectives," signed by David Packard and William Hewlett themselves. This statement might sound idealistic. However, from my firsthand observations of the company and from published accounts of how the company has grown and met the challenges of change, some of which we will see later in this chapter, principles are taken quite seriously.

The achievements of an organization are the result of the combined efforts of each individual in the organization working toward common objectives. These objectives should be realistic, should be clearly understood by everyone in the organization, and should reflect the organization's basic character and personality.

If the organization is to fulfill its objectives, it should strive to meet certain other fundamental requirements:

FIRST, the most capable people available should be selected for each assignment within the organization. Moreover, these people should have the opportunity—through continuing programs of training and education—to upgrade their skills and capabilities. . . .

SECOND, enthusiasm should exist at all levels. People in important management positions should not only be enthusiastic themselves, they should be selected for their ability to engender enthusiasm among their associates. . . .

THIRD, even though an organization is made up of people fully meeting the first two requirements, all levels should work in unison toward common objectives and avoid working at cross purposes if the ultimate in efficiency and achievement is to be obtained.

It has been our policy at Hewlett-Packard not to have a tight military-type organization, but rather, to have overall objectives which are clearly stated and agreed to, and to give people the freedom to work toward those goals in ways they determine best for their own areas of responsibility.[2]

The basic building blocks of a holographic organization are all represented in this statement. When people work toward common objectives, each replicates the company's mission. "Realistic" objectives maintain continuity over time as new projects are undertaken. There is plenty of room for individual initiative, as procedural and job specifications are kept to a minimum. And finally, the organization is defined by its ability to formulate and implement strategy at appropriate levels and marshal resources to meet it challenges. To the greatest extent possible, as a matter of policy, there is no impediment put in the way of creativity, initiative, and responsiveness.

MISSION

The motivating focus of value strategy is strictly and solely the quality of the value relationship between the business and its customers. Since profits are regarded as an outgrowth of how people feel about the quality and significance of the activities for which those products are enablements, the organization's success depends, above all, on its commitment to learning from these value relationships and adapting to these lessons. It is more or less in the position of lead or perish.

We have already seen what may be the epitome of a value-based mission statement in the words of Konosuke Matsushita, the founder of the firm that bears his name. But there are other important examples. Dayton-Hudson, Motorola, Hewlett-Packard, Nordstrom, and Harley-Davidson come to mind as some of the companies we cite as examples throughout these pages.

Dayton-Hudson's mission statement, for example, focuses on providing value to its customers, and then employees, corporate shareholders, and the community, in that order:

Dayton-Hudson Corporation is a diversified retailing company whose business is to serve the American consumer through the retailing of fashion-oriented quality merchandise.

Serving the consumer over time requires skilled and motivated employees, healthy communities in which to operate and maximum long-range profit. We are committed to meaningful and comprehensive employee development, to serving the business, social and cultural needs of our communities and to achieving levels of profitability equivalent to the leading firms in industry.

...The common denominator in serving these constituencies is profit—our reward for serving society well. Long-range profit is thus our major responsibility so that we can continue to serve our constituencies in the future.[3]

This statement illustrates a value-based mission in clear and unmistakable terms. The mission as it is articulated by any one person or other is not the point; the point is the enablement and the business's value relationship to its customers. The mission has the organizational function of defining "internal impetus for growth," as Burgelman calls it,[4] or as we would say, it provides everyone in the organization with a strategy for innovation. It does this in three ways:

- It focuses the organization's members on the enablement and the relationships that support it, clearly establishing what activities the organization selects as being opportunities to which it will assign resources.
- It establishes a balance between what changes the organization will undertake and what the organization will strive to preserve and maintain as critical elements of its survival and continuity.
- It sets out how the organization will define, measure, and achieve the quality of relationship it wants with its customers.

Change and the Mission

In the context of value strategy, however, even the mission itself may change. It can be brought to the point of change by any one of several factors: the business either specializing or expanding its position with regard to the enablement it provides; competitive changes in its markets (price wars, new entrants, a new configuration of the enablement, governmental intervention, etc.); or technical development of new capabilities that affect the enablement. The mission is an expression of that relationship as it really exists; reality or the real conditions of that relationship cannot be molded to fit the mission.

If a value-based mission is to result in holographic organization, however, additional effort is needed beyond its formulation. Everyone must buy into the mission, understand it, and replicate its meanings and implications. The holographic idea is that each person in the organization is capable and given the power to optimize his or her function *for the whole*. That assumes that one person's conception of what constitutes the "whole" bears some resemblance to the image that others in the organization hold.

Adaptability and survivability are thus distributed throughout the organization, down to the most minute of levels. When the mission is distributed and replicated throughout the organization, it can be tested and enacted by more and more people in the organization. When the time comes, then, change can take place meaningfully, responsively, and in accord with actual conditions the business faces and must adapt to.

One company I consulted with is a prime example of how holographic organizational principles play out in practice. Growth was occurring so fast that new people were being added to the payroll, and new services were being developed, it seemed, on a weekly basis. New groupings of people were formed on a project-by-project basis, and titles changed accordingly. But the organization basically moved along rather smoothly. There were some "bumps" along the way, but considering the volatility of the environment these people worked in, change happened remarkably smoothly.

As part of my assignment, I interviewed more than twenty key people in this sixty-person firm. By and large, I found that most of the people I talked to had a finely tuned sense of what the company was about and what its mission or relationship to its clients was. Everyone spoke the same language on that issue. As a result, the changes either made sense to people or were regarded as a fact of life that "keeps things interesting." To many, they were regarded positively as "a sure sign that we're growing and that I'll have a good job for the foreseeable future." The tumult was unsettling to some, but there was a general sense of acceptance and even well-being among most people at all levels.

CULTURE

In the classical forms, the business relates to the changes, without the expectation of having to *internalize* them. In contrast, the value-based organization considers itself to be a participant in the changes. As the status of enablements changes in people's lives, their value relationships change, and accordingly, the business's organization must change. And this does not happen only once in the lifetime of the business. It happens with each change in buyer requirements, with the introduction of each market-shaping innovation, with the maturation of each product category in which the business is involved.

Value strategy adheres to the principle of truly relating to customer requirements, rather than making evaluations based on some internally defined, merely quantitative rubric. In terms of the three "M's" of relating externally, "measurement" is based on quality and is defined strictly in terms of customers' satisfaction with their experience of the product. For instance, in an effort to become more value and customer focused, IBM changed their quality measurement rubric from "bugs per million
lines of code" to "problem days per customer month," pegging quality to customer satisfaction rather than internally defined technical performance.[5]

The "means" value strategy applies to actions tied closely to impressions, lessons, and demands that emanate from direct customer contact. Most companies cannot be in contact with all individuals using their product. So one way companies meet this requirement of direct customer contact is to at least stay in contact with the most demanding customers. Another way is to support user groups or conduct customer focus groups. And neither can all people in the company stay in contact with even these customers. The point is that everyone in the company must know that all the best means are applied toward those relationships.

As Van de Ven points out, "Being exposed face to face with demanding customers . . . increases the likelihood that the action threshold of organizational participants will be triggered and will stimulate them to pay attention to changing environmental conditions or customer needs."[6] Another benefit of high-level customer contact is that innovation is demanded from the top of the organization, ensuring that everyone is directly involved in learning to learn. Those whose energies have not been stimulated by direct contact will be motivated by the demands from the organization's leadership, who are in that kind of direct contact.

As to the four "W's" of internally directed aspects of culture, value strategy calls for low walls, meaningful wages, and different forms of recognition. A career path is often more a matter of meandering around the organization and being assigned to different kinds of projects than it is assumption of ever more impressive-sounding titles. A person's particular contribution is what is valued; and its value is assessed by what the group as a whole accomplishes.

Compensation and recognition follow that performance in such forms as raises, bonuses, and special recognition "chairs." In many value-based companies I have worked with, promotions to more supervisory or administrative positions are not necessarily available or desired. The company's decision makers are explicitly committed to the employees' personal and professional growth, and that suffices for one's "wages."

As to "will," management functions are distributed, and mission-guided autonomy is encouraged. Skills and expertise are seen in the perspective of a creative group dynamic as a resource that is best utilized by being broadened and complemented by different skills, orientations, and areas of expertise. This, of course, results in replication of the mission and a high degree of variety in people's work lives, both components of holographic organizations that value-based strategies aim to support.

Decision makers focus on the problem of who to put on the task of solving a problem: who is best to design a response to an opportunity, to shape resources and an environment in which this group can expeditiously move the program along. This is no easy task, as any decision maker in these pressured, volatile environments will tell you. Still, as one high-tech executive put it, "Maintenance of the culture is totally a function of the energy you pour into it.... The whole driving force behind this is that you don't believe you can have an intensely happy customer unless you have intensely happy employees. You can't have one without the other."[7] The intent of value strategy with regard to culture, then, comes down to keeping the most people possible in direct contact with the essential elements of the business's value relationships and their human context (as well as technical interest and subtleties). The organization provides the internal incentives to do so, and it provides an environment in which innovation can be identified, initiated, and pursued. Not all programs will follow through to completion, but people in these organizations know that at least they will be able to pursue an idea to the point where an honest evaluation can be made. In most cases, this is all people ask for.

NOTES

1. Andrew H. Van de Ven, "Central Problems in the Management of Innovation," *Management Science* 32, no. 5 (May 1986): 596.

2. William G. Ouchi, *Theory Z: How American Business Can Meet the Japanese Challenge* (Reading, Mass.: Addison-Wesley, 1981), pp. 225–226.

3. Ibid., p. 234.

4. Robert A. Burgelman, "Corporate Entrepreneurship and Strategic Management: Insights from a Process Study," *Management Science* 29, no. 12 (December 1983): 1353.

5. Bruce C. P. Rayner, "A Blueprint for Competition," *Electronic Business*, March 18, 1991, p. 46.

6. Van de Ven, "Central Problems in the Management of Innovation," p. 596.

7. Elizabeth B. Baatz, "The Changing Face of the Organization," *Electronic Business*, March 18, 1991, p. 62.

11

Capital and Management in Value Strategy

CAPITAL

Capital provides a means of payment for a business's new directions. At a very minimum, *new directions* means not mere repetition. The term can entail expanding facilities, changing organization and/or production methods, or moving into new product innovations or new product ventures. But *new* means a business undertakes something its current mode of operation does not encompass.

Capital is the business's means to be able to act on an opportunity. Decisions about the use of capital must encompass the vision and anticipation of there being further transactions that meet requirements for providing attractive enablements to buyers.

Hewlett-Packard's Corporate Statement again demonstrates a value-based understanding of capital as a component of organizational strategy:

In our economic system, the profit we generate from our operations is the ultimate source of the funds we need to prosper and grow. It is the one absolutely essential measure of our corporate performance over the long term....

Our long-standing policy has been to reinvest most of our profits and to depend on this reinvestment, plus funds from employee stock purchases and other cash flow items, to finance our growth. This can be achieved if our return on net worth is roughly equal to our sales growth rate. We must strive to reach this goal every year without limiting our efforts to attain our other objectives.

Meeting our profit objective requires that we design and develop each and every product so that it is considered a good value by our customers, yet is priced to include an adequate profit. Maintaining this competitiveness in the marketplace also requires that we perform our manufacturing, marketing and administrative functions as economically as possible.

Profit is the responsibility of all.[1]

Business Capital Versus Entrepreneurial Capital

This is not to say value-based capital strategy tries to emulate entrepreneurial situations within established companies. Value strategy becomes necessary when businesses have established value relationships with customers. Thus, as Harold Geneen would say, such a company is not in a position to "bet the store" on a single idea or gamble its corporate existence away on a single innovation. Entrepreneurs, on the other hand, seek to establish a new enablement, innovation, or idea. They have no choice but to "bet the store."

Since ongoing businesses have a responsibility to their existing customers (not to mention other stakeholders, such as employees, shareholders, and the communities they serve), capital decisions are made more conservatively. Generally, programs that are capitalized gravitate toward these kinds of situations:

- The innovation or new enablement meets a widely held desire and/ or frequently used enablement.

- It is, or has the potential to become, an "attractor" product or is closely associated with one. Thus, it integrates (several or many) other value relationships in the course of its use (such as the automobile).

- It requires the use, coordination, and multiplication of capital to be produced.

- It has a meaningful but limited life span, so reinvestment on the part of other buyers is necessary.

One has only to think of the inventions that have established themselves in the last decade to see how these play out in fact. The VCR, for instance, bridged the gap between two frequently used enablements: the television and motion picture entertainment, integrating them into a new yet somehow familiar form. It spawned many subsidiary products and services, from the now ubiquitous video store to the camcorder. The product lasts for a long time, but upgrades have made repurchase attractive—with no end in sight.

FORMS OF CAPITAL

We have already discussed how capital functions for the business in chapter 7. Our focus is thus on a different aspect of the idea of capital. Here we want to set out how changing customer demands and the incessant pressure of turnover changes (1) how we have to look at capital and (2) what we have to consider as being the capital that is available to invest in an opportunity.

In particular, we want to show that capital must be considered as a fund of *all* resources at the disposal of decision makers to undertake and guide change. Two sources of capital have been largely overlooked by decision makers in business as well as in the political and academic economic arena: labor as capital and social capital.

Labor and Employees as Capital

Value strategy has a far different view of what constitutes capital than does its classical counterparts. *Labor* here refers to the energies and attention people apply to tasks that result in the business's products and services. As most classical writers, from Eugen Bohm-Bawerk to Joseph Schumpeter, present the picture, labor is not considered to be capital that enables a business to grow and change. Classical strategies deny that labor is a fund of capital because management fully reimburses labor in the form of wages, which immediately depletes whatever fund has been accumulated.

In their view, wages are not the only things that have to be considered as depleting the fund of capital available for growth and change. Today, businesses provide for other aspects of the workers' well-being: disability compensation, social security and/or pension payments, and health insurance, to name a few. Any way that labor might be considered as capital on those terms is fully canceled by these contributions to workers' well-being since these payments draw the funds that would otherwise be available for new investment down to zero.

Then, in another way, in comparison with machinery, or "capital equipment," as it is called, labor again seems to fall short as a fund of capital for business. Machinery qualifies as a repository for capital as long as it still has a productive life within an ongoing, profitable value relationship. Labor, on the other hand, more or less works on a pay-as-you-go basis. In fact, when training is considered, labor is actually a cost against capital for an extended period of time. So it looks as though labor is not a good candidate as a source or repository of capital for a business. Labor only creates expenditures in the forms of wages, benefits, and training.

But staying on the edge of innovation in the context of value relationships and in the face of turnover reverses the relative status of equipment and labor as forms of capital. While machines merely spend the capital invested in them over successive production cycles, labor actually accumulates capital for the business in the form of their growing experience and deepening knowledge of the processes, materials, and relationships required to produce the business's products and services. Thus, from the moment the business begins to respond to its value relationships in the form of innovations, labor assumes the form of capital.

Labor also provides the significant bridge between the old form of the product and the new. Whereas machinery will be scrapped, again becoming a 100 percent cost factor, labor can adapt to the new situation. In fact, by virtue of its knowledge, experience, abilities, and limitations, the quality of labor's involvement, knowledge, and initiative will determine what kind of equipment will have to be purchased and the extent to which it will be used effectively.

In this role, labor is a fund for future productivity and becomes a direct capital contributor. Payments made to labor in the form of wages are actually installment payments to an annuity, redeemable with interest when the time comes for devising and implementing change. In fact, as realized by decision makers at Hewlett-Packard, Dayton-Hudson, Xerox Corporation, and other companies in the forefront of today's business world, the higher the rate of turnover, the greater premium there is to the labor form of capital.

But then labor can serve in this capacity only when the kinds of holographic organizational principles we have been emphasizing are put into practice. A labor force that is denied any of the four holographic organizational principles—requisite variety, redundancy of functions, learning to learn, limited specification—will not have the tools to participate in this process. So the classical strategists perpetuate a self-fulfilling prophesy of labor intransigence by treating labor in ways that foreclose on their capital-producing capacities. Regimented, segmented, and disenfranchised laborers in mass production lines will have neither the knowledge nor the motivation to move away from the familiar and the comfortable to what may be new and threatening.

Social Capital

Social capital is another form of capital not acknowledged by the classical pundits. In their view, social expenditures for infrastructure such as roads, bridges, and sewer systems and services such as public education, health insurance, police, and fire are drains on capital in the form of taxes that deplete funds available for reinvestment, takeovers, and buyouts. While these public expenditures are improvements and enhancements to people's life-styles that business profits make possible, they do not act as capital that contributes to businesses' ability to make profits.

But once again, this is true only if businesses make the same products over and over again. Businesses are now discovering the true value of education as a form of social capital, for instance. And they're learning it the hard way: Because of the failure of our underfunded, poorly administered public school systems, many businesses have to invest large sums of money to upgrade the basic skills—reading, writing, elementary mathematics—of their workers so they can perform the tasks that are basic and necessary in today's competitive environment. On another front, poor roads and bridges add millions of dollars to delivery costs, which drains capital needed for investment in innovation.

The validity of the idea of social capital changes as soon as we assert that the purpose of a business is to provide, maintain, and enhance enablements that enrich people's lives. Since innovation is not a luxury, but an absolute turnover-driven necessity of business life, these forms of public expenditure must be seen in a new light. Not only do these expenditures support and enhance the current conditions of value re- lationships (roads for an economy dependent on automobiles; public education for an economy that requires literacy and knowledge), but they also lessen the amount of money a business has to spend in order to sell its products, or they directly subsidize the capitalization necessary to accomplish its ends.

Social expenditures such as these are means of payment for business to do its job. They constitute a fund of resources that are advanced to them by the public through socially mandated agencies. Business is short- sighted in any attempt to curtail the ability of the society to provide for these essential alternate forms of capital; and society, on the other hand, is shortsighted if it overtaxes a business, depleting its private capital and thus curtailing its ability to participate in its specialty: producing valued enablements. To expand on Hewlett-Packard's idea about its own prof- itability, providing for adequate social capital is truly the responsibility of all, business decision maker and citizen alike.

MANAGEMENT

In value strategy, the rule about management is, keep it *flat*. Managers are kept close to the customer. In fact, the more senior the manager, the more oriented toward customer contact and instilling the urgency of customers' requirements in the organization he or she is. Middle managers are needed when complex tasks are required of many people. Their job is to gather all necessary information from whatever sources are available, including customers, and bring decisions into focus in a timely fashion. They also ensure that organizational resources are available, while organizational impediments are cleared away.

Function Versus Position

The management component of value strategy is based on the holographic principle of minimizing the number of different management levels by upgrading the *functions* of each position, adding variety and redundancy of functions, throughout the organization. "Redundancy" does not mean mere repetition and overlap. It means each job is enriched with depth, complexity, and responsibility rather than narrowed down to one operation or concentration of specialization and authority. Hewlett-Packard expresses this orientation this way.

In discussing HP operating policies, we often refer to the concept of "management by objective." By this we mean that insofar as possible each individual at each level in the organization should make his or her own plans to achieve company objectives and goals. After receiving supervisory approval, each individual should be given a wide degree of freedom to work within the limitations imposed by these plans and by our general corporate policies. Finally, each person's performance should be judged on the basis of how well these individually established goals have been achieved.
  ... Thus a primary HP management responsibility is communication and mutual understanding. Conversely, employees must take sufficient interest in their work to want to plan it, to propose new solutions to old problems, to stick their necks out when they have something to contribute.[2]

In value strategy, managers do not limit people's initiative with regard to approved projects and programs. Rather, consistent with holographic principles, managers have the role of providing for organizational cohesion and vision while they encourage drive and initiative. They also provide resources in a timely way to enable all participants to respond meaningfully to the value relation while, at the same time, fostering the sense that the company is supporting their efforts.

The managerial imperative here is highly *interpersonal* rather than capital, technical, or expertise oriented. At the highest levels, management acts as the final decision maker on projects and product decisions, based on a combination of cohesion and continuity in the company, on the one hand, and on the suitability of the solution for meeting customer requirements, on the other. On lower levels, management acts as broker or facilitator, ensuring that projects get a full hearing and once set in motion, get executed properly.

We will not venture into any more depth on this subject here, since sorting out these issues, a difficult job at best, is better discussed under the heading of value production strategy, in chapters 12 through 14.

Here we can only say that in a value organization strategy the role of management is not enforcement of the rules, structures, and standards but rather the evocation of the most effective production and participation of everyone involved.

In some circles, this has been called the "web of management structure," substituting for the "pyramid" structure of classical organizations.[3] This is as good an image as any, signifying that managers act like filaments in a web that captures ideas, abilities, and energies in order to bring them together in a single endeavor.

Management and Capital

One problem for managers in value strategy is that they must compete for capital. By virtue of its power of judgment and evaluation, capital-based decision making pervasively injects its influence into management prerogatives. Managers must prove their ability to manage and augment that capital against what others are able to do. Capital decision makers require managers to prove their knowledge of the business's value relationships, to demonstrate their capacity to manage its uncertainties.

To fully grasp the dynamics of this relationship, we also must remember that both capital and management are involved in an enterprise to bring about something that does not yet exist. We cannot underestimate the significance of this fact. On the one hand, capital is not applied toward repetitive activity, so it is truly dependent on management's hands-on experience and analytical insight to bring about its goals. Yet management, full of energy and determination, can only dream about what it imagines it can do without the availability of capital. Neither would be *actors*, in terms of the business's value relationships, without the other.

So this confrontation is not one of servitude where one has absolute life and death power and the other must yield to it. It is an ambiguous relationship where the goals and objectives are shared, and the terms of evaluation are mutually agreed on in advance of the actions taken. And neither is this confrontation simply a contest of opposing wills. If management and capital merely confronted one another in this manner, they would tend to cancel one another out, and nothing at all would ensue. We know for a fact, from direct observation, that when this kind of thing does happen, nothing gets built. We also know from the evidence of successful products and services all around us that management and capital do work together to make things happen.

We are thus left with a thoroughly ambiguous relationship. It is pretty clear that in terms of their intrinsic natures and positions in, and with regard to, the value relationship, managers and capital decision makers confront one another at every turn. Yet it is also clear that within the value relationship there is management only to the extent that there is capital, and vice versa. It is an alliance, not a marriage: Capital is management's means of payment; management is capital's means of expansion. Capital is management's judge; management is capital's means. They must come together if a value relationship is to develop at all. Capital decision makers thus dictate, but management decides. Capital decision makers believe there can be a value relationship if, and only if, management does the work to shape and define it.

VALUE STRATEGY AND THE ORGANIZATION

We originally defined *strategy* as a way to comprehend change in the business's core relationships so as to optimize its chances for success in engaging emergent challenges, adapting today's understandings to tomorrow's demands. In detailing the tenets of a value organization strategy, we see what this definition means in an operational sense: In a value organization strategy, no component of the organization takes precedence over the maintenance and enhancement of the business's essential value relationships.

The intent of value strategy is that organizational structure be able to meet the challenges of change and turnover. The organization's structure will serve as a starting point from out of which meaningful, incremental adaptations are undertaken at the appropriate level of decision and action. The only way this can be done is by incorporating the holographic principles in which each member is trusted, encouraged, and recognized for the ability to internalize and embody the strategy of the whole organization. Within the guidelines of the company's mission and culture, each person adopts his or her own version of autonomous strategic behavior and carries it out in accord with others.

Van de Ven cites three organizational characteristics that support this kind of orientation:

1. *Authenticity.* The company's decision makers embody the company's ideals visibly and consistently. For instance, if a company is committed to innovation, it will find a way to pursue and support valid ideas even if the risk is great. Authenticity gives all members of the organization a firm sense that the company's promises and its realities jibe and can be believed over the long term and through tough times.

2. *Flexibility.* The company's decision makers listen. Ideas are not passed over because they come from untitled sources. In fact, titled managers are not in any way expected to originate all innovations, but they are responsible for recognizing good ideas. Inner walls

are low; communication is truly open. When companies exhibit this trait, employees' enthusiasm is encouraged, and larger increments of change will be accepted.

3. *Functionality.* The company's decision makers are capable of recognizing, supporting, and implementing ideas that work. This gives people in the company the feeling that changes can be undertaken successfully and that the changes that are chosen are likely to succeed.[4]

A receptiveness to, and confidence in, the authenticity, flexibility, and functionality of the company's decision-making processes—a process that includes all levels of the company's membership—allows this basic organizational change to take place. It encourages the ability of everyone in the organization to contribute to and to respond to change with directed, focused, and self-initiated actions.

The ultimate goal of value strategy, then, is to encourage the development of holographic organizations and autonomous strategic behavior in which the business is able to meet the demands of its essential value relationships. Everyone has a stake, not in the structure, but in the ability to change the structure to get the job done. The strategy becomes the structure.

Naturally, no one wants to undertake the kind of wrenching changes we are talking about here. But to deal with the forces of changing customer demands and market turnover, businesses often have no other choice. To make these changes feasible and acceptable requires the kind of holographic approach to organization we have outlined. We can boil down the tenets of value organization strategy to these points:

• Value strategy emanates from the nature and dynamic of the value relationship—and nothing else. The people in the organization must be tied to, and focused on, the business's essential relationships, not "perks," status, position, or pay relative to someone else's.

• Value strategy trends away from centrally conceptualized organizational superstructure and is more dependent on interpersonal understanding and insight.

• Value strategy does not depend on abstract goals, such as market share or return on equity. It is based on real-life, real-time value relationships with real customers.

• Profit, market share, and return on equity are necessary for the survival of a business. But they are measures of the success of that strategy only after the fact. Most of the time they are not goals in and of themselves that exclude or override all other considerations. There are times when a concentration on the bottom line is necessary, but those times have to pass to allow a customer-focused value strategy to reemerge and renew the organization.

• Value strategy envisions a process that *generates* change as well as one that conceives of responses to change. Change is the natural and logical outcome of a process in which formulating and implementing strategy are the responsibility of everyone in the company.

NOTES

1. William G. Ouchi, *Theory Z: How American Business Can Meet the Japanese Challenge* (Reading, Mass.: Addison-Wesley, 1981), pp. 226–227.

2. Ibid., pp. 231–232.

3. See, for instance, John Holusha, "Grace Pastiak's 'Web of Inclusion,' " *New York Times*, May 5, 1991, sec. 3, p. 1.

4. Andrew H. Van de Ven, "Central Problems in the Management of Innovation," *Management Science* 32, no. 5 (May 1986): 603.

12

Production and the Value Relationship

In this chapter and the remaining three, we shift our focus from the broad reach of organization strategy to the narrower sphere of production. In a sense, everything we have said about strategy up to this point is preliminary: It all points to how the business will make the decisions and marshal resources in order to produce enablements for its customers. But, as anyone who has made decisions about production will appreciate, organizational strategy and production strategy are tightly connected to one another.

To understand how organizational strategy and production strategy interact, it is useful to refer to our organism image. Organization strategy is analogous to an organism's morphology—its body type, including its limbs, lungs, and digestive tract. The organism's body shape and form determine how it will accomplish its essential life functions of locomotion, respiration, and digestion. Similarly, an organization strategy organizes the business's members into a form that determines how it will conduct its essential function of production.

In nature, the connection between body and action is a reciprocal, two-way relationship. The organism devises survival strategies that uses its body—limbs, lungs, and digestive tract—in certain ways in order to provide for that body's continued life. Birds fly to catch prey; chameleons camouflage themselves for protection and to avoid their prey's premature detection of danger.

Similarly, a business devises a production strategy to use its organization in order to maximize its effectiveness in providing enablements that yield profits—the lifeblood of the business. So a business's production strategy deploys the talents and energies of the members of the organization in order to preserve the business and to enable it to thrive in its markets.

Thus the focus of our attention in this chapter and following ones will be to see what effect the value relationship and the effects of turnover have on an organization's production strategy. Just as a biologist would not attempt to prescribe how an organism *should* live in its environment, we will not attempt to prescribe how a business should operate in its markets.

What we will do, however, is to show how the changes wrought by the onset of turnover and world-class competition have changed the ecological balance. So organizations have to develop a new outlook on their production processes, a new strategy for production that accounts for volatility, change, and constant market disruption.

To fully appreciate the pressures on production in today's businesses, we have to keep two things in mind: First, the life span of a product or service is marked off in increments of cycles of use (hours, days, months, or maybe years). There are few products or services that can remain the same year after year because they satisfy eternally repetitious "human needs." A business can no longer presume that it can just keep "stamping out" the same product or performing the same service in the same way, quarter after quarter.

Second, there is nothing natural or intrinsically necessary about any product's success. The buyer wants to carry out an interaction that is enabled by a product. Whether or not a particular product is available is of little cosmic concern as long as a substitute or alternative is available. Loyalty to the product itself, or to a brand name, is thin at best and, very likely, nonexistent.[1] There is no evidence to support an assumption that a product that was once valued will be in the future. In fact, market forces conspire to cancel whatever value there was in the previous transaction.

At its best, a product or service presents an opportunity for a business to enter into a relationship with a buyer. A business's role is to create value, and as we have seen, that means making a particular enablement convenient, accessible, and meaningful to a buyer. When decision makers realize this, the definition of production becomes the *process* of creating relationships and not making just things. Production truly begins when the power of the business's members is unleashed so as to take all actions necessary to meet these demands.

This puts the business in a paradoxical situation. On the one hand, it has itself, its existence, survival, and profitability at stake. Any organization, after all, seeks long-term viability and desires some measure of equilibrium and balance. Yet it can remain viable only by being willing and able to transform itself in response to its customers' demands and turnover. To survive, the business must be a focal point for change. People in the organization must decide to undertake the changes that are not immediately necessary, to anticipate the conditions new demands are likely to bring about in the future. They must, in other words, generate change.

Strategy is the process by which decision makers both accept and modulate change in the course of fulfilling requirements for maintaining ongoing value relationships. It is a process in which decision makers have to "think on their feet" even as the ground shifts beneath them.

GENERAL CHARACTERISTICS OF PRODUCTION

In general, these are the characteristics that define production:

1. Production begins the moment the organization must respond to the value relationship it has set in motion by its products and/or services, or when there is an opportunity to make an enablement available to a more or less definable group of potential or known buyers.

Production encompasses all business actions that enable a business to participate in its value relationships. It comprises all actions that create conditions, relations, and products or services that have the potential to create value by means of transactions with buyers. This includes all actions the business undertakes with regard to its products (e.g., equipment, design, materials, vendors) and its organization (e.g., personnel, organization, compensation) that have anything at all to do with supporting and enhancing its value relationships.

2. If we understand the term *work* to designate any effort people expend while engaged in a purposeful activity, then production is a specialized kind of work. Production is not the kind of work that makes specific things for individuals; that is "craft." A craftsman might undertake a project to make a violin just for himself, for example, regardless of whether or not there was a buyer envisioned. Production, however, always envisions a pool of buyers whether or not it is there in fact.

3. Thus, production is always structured by influences and directions that are imposed on decision makers from extrinsic sources. Capital-based decisions, as we saw in chapter 7, allocate financial resources based on reading and interpreting the pace and direction of socioeconomic conditions and the state and pace of market turnover. Those decisions determine the time frame and resource pool in which production will work.

Production is then shaped and guided by management. As we saw earlier, the orientation and motivating focus of management determine the specific controls that will be applied to any ongoing operation and also set out the criteria by means of which operations are measured and evaluated. These include standards of performance, compensation, recognition, and so on.

Production is also shaped by markets. The demographic characteristics of current and potential buyers—income, life-style, education—as well as the factors of competition and turnover determine the pace, diversity, and style production will assume.

Production is structured by the materials used—the human and technical resources, especially the quality and quantity of personnel, available to carry out the action—and by the relationships the business maintains within its domain (of suppliers, supporters, and competitors).

Finally, production reflects the condition of the society in general. Production is either helped by the society's advancing technical, sociological, educational, and communications capabilities as well as its interpersonal qualities, such as its acceptance of cultural and/or racial diversity, or it is hindered by society's shortcomings in these areas.

4. Production always begins in an environment of change, and it always results in change. Of course, production supports existing products and does involve repetitious output for periods of time. But when a business faces turnover in its markets and domain, even if it is involved with producing commodities year after year, it does not escape the need to undertake change. Even if demand for its products remains stable, it is doubtful that the inner workings of the business's production process will be left untouched. New manufacturing technologies; new products in its markets; new financial, regulatory, or environmental conditions— all exert pressures that bring even the most repetitious of businesses face to face with change.

5. Production is only undertaken when the business as a whole can undertake it, when the necessary actions are within the means and capabilities of the business as a whole. Production is only undertaken when it is judged that this undertaking can be sustained and can be a life-giving activity for the whole business. However, the scale of production, as well as its composition and structure, will reflect the resources a business is able to apply to it, primarily as dictated by profits and cash flow.

PRODUCTION AND THE VALUE RELATIONSHIP

As we saw earlier, changing customer demands and turnover require that decision makers shift the focus and intent of organizational strategy toward the basic relational and interactive components of a business's life. This holds true at the level of production as well.

As we noted in the first chapter, value is only created when buyers can count on an enablement's being available to support their chosen life activities (when buyers decide to continue to do word processing and accounting on a personal computer, for example); and profits only ensue when this product becomes an integral part of the buyers' desired (or required) interactions in their world and is subsequently purchased by large numbers of people repeatedly.

While a product is in production, therefore, it does not yet have value. A product is only a thing (or a service) among other things that a business offers in hope of creating value. If the product has established itself as a viable and desirable form of an enablement, then it is likely that it will have value. It will create profits if it is purchased by a sufficient number of buyers. But that is not by any means guaranteed. There may indeed be a product packaged up and ready to go out the door, but a new value relationship is not yet established, or a continuing value relationship is not yet sustained or enhanced. The cycle that creates value is not yet complete. This conclusion has remarkable consequences for how decision makers must approach production.

For one thing, the production process must serve customers. Customers drive decisions, and markets determine priorities because competitors offer attractive alternatives and new products reshape the meaning, status, and configuration of enablements. Production is the process in which the business responds to changes and challenges posed by the relationship it wants with its customers. Decision makers must concentrate their attention on how their organization goes about producing the occasions during which it will make and consolidate viable value relationships with existing and potential customers.

The business of today is not a dictatorial monolith that compels allegiance by virtue of the control it exercises. The decisions as to what needs to be produced, the criteria for incorporation and acceptance, and the very image of what the enablement is supposed to be and therefore what kind of business a buyer wants as a value partner are all determined outside the business's confines, in the give and take of a buyer's own value process. As in any relationship, the business must deal with incomplete knowledge, unproven hunches about its value relationships. At some level of the endeavor, at some stage in the production process, decision makers must take the plunge into the untested waters of customers' desires, requirements, and demands.

These are not conditions that are amenable to "rational," centralized, and hierarchical controls. Rather than carrying out a centrally articulated goal, the business operates on the basis of what is called "fuzzy logic"— or on the basis of what Gareth Morgan cites as a form of "negative feedback model."[2] Participants aim for the goal, make mistakes, and correct them, in a continuing sequence that approaches, but never quite achieves, perfection.

It is not that perfection in some limited area or operation is not possible. It is rather that, in the mode of "learning to learn" that we talked about earlier, decision makers also have to change the conception of their goals, methods, and roles. Thus, a new process of approximation and approach must be fashioned. We'll talk more about this process in the next chapter, where we'll detail what Morgan calls "double loop learning,"[3] a process that goes beyond training in new techniques to examine the very basis and rationale for decisions.

In this kind of situation, decision makers find that despite their comprehension of the business's relationship to its customers and the company's excellent status in its markets, it can no longer dictate what will constitute the content and methods of production. The most meaningful and useful comprehension of what customers want and markets mandate as standard practice and quality actually emerges from production.

Value strategy at the level of production constitutes a wholesale adoption on the part of the business of the terms, requirements, and conditions of the value relationship, not as it is, but as it is envisioned. Any specific solution that production undertakes is neither anticipated nor inevitable. At this moment, everyone in the organization is facing a world of possibilities, defined only by some known parameters from its previous experience in that relationship. The value relationship demands action in the face of the uncertainty of change, and the real and present threat of failure. Business is not an undertaking for the fainthearted.

One could adopt the attitude that the value relationship poses to the business an impossible task, full of frustration and heartache; but it also presents the right kind of people and the right kind of organization with a highly charged arena that invites actions of initiative and inventiveness that are intensely challenging even if they are only potentially rewarding.

In light of this, value strategy provides a way to capitalize on the existence of an ongoing value relationship. Just as any relationship requires time and attention, so does the value relationship. Relationships are also the most rewarding and enriching aspects of our lives. So it is with businesses as well. The value relationship forms a recognizable and motivating frame of reference. It takes on the role of an adopted end to which all available means are applied.

Value strategy highlights those aspects of the relationship that do motivate people and uses them to leverage the talents and energies of everyone in the organization.

QUALITY: THE GOAL OF PRODUCTION

As we have said, a product or service engages a buyer through its quality. The quality of the product or service determines whether the experience of that enablement is positive or is at least worth the effort. It is the quality of the experience itself, not any extrinsic image making, guarantees, or other gimmicks, that reinforces a positive outcome, the repurchasing of the product, and so creates value. Thus, a value-based strategy for production envisions all actions necessary to ensure (or maximize chances) that value will be created throughout the course of the transaction, that each product meets the highest standards of quality possible. Once this insight is realized, it becomes clear that the very ideas of production, value, and quality are inextricably linked.

A product or service only creates value when buyers project and anticipate using it in their ongoing life activities. Production must build in what customers anticipate as being the standard in their projections, or else the product will not be used again.

This conception of value changes some of the typical ways quality is understood. For instance, quality is often thought of as "zero defects," meaning that a product is not shipped out the door, or does not move to the next stage of production, if it contains a defect. This is always a necessary, and sometimes a sufficient, aspect of quality. But it would only suffice as a definition of quality in capital-based strategies that are concerned with eliminating rework and reducing scrap. Within a value relationship, quality must meet the standards established for its use in real-life situations and nothing less.

Quality is not just a matter of adding features or benefits to a product or service, either. This "value-added" approach may well serve to differentiate a product for a time or establish a platform on which to support high prices (and margins), as is the case with Detroit's strategy with luxury cars. But this approach only works in management-based, defensive strategies where market share is purchased with incentives, and profits are propped up by extrinsic gadgetry. As Detroit has slowly learned, quality means creating the experience of the activity that buyers want.

Establishing a "customer service" department that is dedicated to handling complaints or answering questions that accompanying documentation doesn't address is a stopgap measure. It is not a substitute for full participation in the value relationship throughout all phases of production. In fact, dependence on such after-sale service often presents a serious barrier to developing a value relationship—no matter how friendly, courteous, and deferential the service representatives might be.

General Motors is becoming aware of this and is genuinely taking the kinds of actions that reflect this new understanding of quality. Saturn is the new division General Motors established with the goal of starting afresh with a new commitment to quality in production. In May 1991, nearly 2,000 brand-new Saturn cars were recalled owing to the fact that factory-installed antifreeze would have prematurely corroded engines. Rather than merely replacing the antifreeze, Saturn made the decision to replace the car for all 1,836 customers involved.

As *Business Week* reported, "Saturn's offer . . . is almost unheard of in an industry rife with recalls."[4] Saturn is now using the incident to bolster and support General Motors' claim to being dedicated to quality. A vice-president of the company stated that the company has instructed its salespeople to mention the recall and how Saturn is handling it.

Quality summarizes how the interactive aspects of the product's presentation are carried through in the course of the buyer's transaction and experience with it. The awareness of the buyer's likely perceptions and emotional response during the interaction with the product must be built into the process, from the moment of the product's conception and then executed throughout its development.

Production thus ensures quality by anticipating and fulfilling the criteria by which buyers judge the product in the course of use in daily life. This means:

1. The product or service will, as Mazda has expressed it in its advertisements, "feel right." In the case of products, the design will be appropriate, clear, and intelligible; the buttons or keys of an instrument will feel good as they move, and displays will be easy to read; the machine will respond quickly to commands; the intervals between service will be reasonable or unexpectedly long. For services, the interactions will have a cordial, confidence-building quality to them and will provide support and comfort to the buyer.

2. The product or service will approach the enablement with imagination, energy, empathy, and expansiveness. In terms of products, this means the enablement will be supported in such a way that it expands people's capabilities and does not intimidate them. This is the difference between Apple's approach to personal computers versus IBM's in the early years. Apple was a brash, young, chaotic start-up that, in many respects, had no business surviving with the "big guys" like IBM. It did survive because of that one quality, "user friendliness," that made Apple computers fun to use.

   As far as services are concerned, Nordstrom leads the way as an exemplar in retailing. Its policy of satisfying the customer is legendary. Door-to-door delivery and no-questions-asked returns are standard. If a customer wants something that Nordstrom doesn't have, salespeople have been known to go to another store and buy it for the customer. The idea is that meeting the customer's requirements for service is an opportunity, not an obligation. This delivery philosophy is combined with tight inventory controls and operating efficiencies. The results in terms of the bottom line validate this approach: While other department stores were struggling with losses or minuscule growth in the recession of 1991, Nordstrom's first-quarter profits rose a startling 95 percent to $26 million, on sales of $611 million.[5]

3. Quality exemplifies worthwhile social values, and the company has to be known for supporting them. This aspect of quality reinforces the idea in every buyer's mind that the company takes seriously the fact that it is involved in a relationship for which it bears responsibility.

Certainly Exxon's experience with the *Exxon Valdez* disaster on March 24, 1990, proves that a powerful company can get away with taking a callous position with regard to its social responsibilities (although it did spend millions in a reluctant attempt to clean up the spill, prodded every step of the way by public opinion and the government).

But to balance this there is the nearly mythic example of an American company standing up to be counted for quality in Johnson & Johnson's handling of the Tylenol scare. In October 1982, someone laced selected bottles of Tylenol with the lethal substance strychnine. Rather than try to cover up the story or localize the problem, Johnson & Johnson took all Tylenol capsules off the shelves nationwide. The company also immediately introduced "tamper-proof" packaging—an innovation that set a new standard others in the over-the-counter drug trade had to follow. People were speculating that the incident would mark the end of the brand, if not Johnson & Johnson's product, but the company's unhesitating response, demonstrating a total commitment to quality, won it praise and added trust instead.

What all of these aspects of quality point to is that the enablement contributes to a bright future for people who engage in it. And this is not a matter of advertising claims, splashed across a television screen in vivid colors, hard bodies, and loud music. It is rather that by means of a buyer's experience with the product, new possibilities are opened up: Time is saved; new kinds of sights and sounds can be sensed; new places can be explored; some pains and discomfort can be alleviated at reasonable costs. And there is a gain in some sense of security and well-being.

VALUE STRATEGY AND PRODUCTION: CONTEXT AND PRESUPPOSITIONS

The aim of a value production strategy, as we will see in the chapters that follow, is to develop and sustain a process in which these aspects of quality are infused in each step of the process and become a concern to each participant. This is possible, as some of the companies cited here demonstrate, when it is firmly kept in mind that a company's primary job is to produce a value relationship that exhibits integrity, innovativeness, and energy.

A consensus is emerging about the characteristics of companies and working groups that contribute to quality, value-creating production. These conclusions, culled from creative business decision makers and researchers in the field, can help us to frame the solution constructively.

1. Organizations are considered to be what Robert Burgelman calls "opportunity structures"[6] rather than routine-enforcing machines. What is called for is for organizations to produce "uninhibiting environments"[7] that encourage and demand dynamic learning— "learning to learn" behavior, that is a key feature of the holographic, value-based organization strategy.

2. These organizations are structured to be highly interactive so as to promote solutions, not expertise. This points to a strategy that optimizes the organization's application of human capital. To do this, boundaries are kept low and communications opportunities are multiplied and accelerated by using organizational and/or technical aids such as teleconferencing and interactive computing. Energy and inventiveness are applied in the use of the organization's resources.

3. Organizations are flatter, with less, little, or no hierarchy. The role of the organization is to marshal resources, not divide responsibilities.[8] The attention of organizational leaders is focused on ensuring that the production process does flow.

4. Technology provides support to the people who make decisions. It performs the functions too precise, too repetitious, too dangerous for humans. Technology is also used to generate detailed information, presented and collated in a variety of formats that can lead to decisions. People, on the other hand, are positioned for the contributions they can make of ideas and personalities as well as for their ability to perform a specific operation.

5. Managers set high standards and expectations for developing new ideas. "Kaleidoscopic thinking," as Rosabeth Moss Kanter calls it, is encouraged.[9] Interactions geared to problem solving and innovation are fostered across departmental boundaries. Managers are attuned to recognizing the potential value of new ideas and are expected to find ways to leverage the organization's resources so they bear fruit.

With these kinds of facilitating concepts in mind, decision makers can proceed to address the details of a value production strategy.

NOTES

1. See "What's in a Name? Less and Less," *Business Week*, July 8, 1991, pp. 66–67.

2. Gareth Morgan, *Images of Organization* (Newbury Park, Calif.: Sage, 1986), pp. 84–87.

3. Ibid., p. 88; see also Figure 13.2, below.

4. "Getting Mileage From a Recall," *Business Week*, May 27, 1991, pp. 38–39.

5. Ibid., p. 47.

6. Robert A. Burgelman, "Corporate Entrepreneurship and Strategic Management: Insights from a Process Study," *Management Science* 29, no. 12 (December 1983): 1353.

7. Robert D. Russel, "How Organizational Culture Can Help to Institutionalize the Spirit of Innovation in Entrepreneurial Ventures," *Journal of Organizational Change Management* 2, no. 3 (1989): 10.

8. Hirotaka Takeuchi and Ikjiro Nonaka, "The New Product Development Game," *Harvard Business Review*, January-February 1986, p. 141.

9. Rosabeth Moss Kanter, "When a Thousand Flowers Bloom: Structural, Collective and Social Conditions for Innovation in Organization," in *Research in Organizational Behavior*, vol. 10, Barry M. Staw and L. L. Cummings, eds. (Greenwich, Conn.: JAI Press, 1988), p. 175.

13

Producing for Value

Value production strategy ensures that all the company's resources, experience, and intelligence are brought to bear in a timely fashion on its value relationships, assuring the necessary talents, energy, and concentration are applied to those relationships.

This conception of production demands that decision makers forge a new perspective on what happens when the business's resources are marshaled into action. The old terms of *control* and *productivity* are useful as measurements of what has already taken place. But when the relationship with customers is the object of attention, these terms are hardly indicative of what transpires now, day to day, position by position, hour by hour, in these dynamic interactions. To monitor and assess the status of its value relationships during the course of production, managers have to pay attention to what we call the "flow of value" or "value flow" progressing through the whole organization.

PRODUCTION AS THE FLOW OF VALUE

Value strategy conceives of production as the flow of value, as a stream of energy shaped by customers' demands that enters the business through "contact points" in the organization. From these points, the demand then flows further into the organization, being assimilated and generating responses as it goes. As it flows on through the organization, this energy is channeled through a matrix of talents, skills, and supporting technologies. These talents apply qualitatively different types of attention to that flow, so that it is transformed from being a problem, opportunity, or challenge into a product or service that meets customer requirements and expectations.

First, we want to detail the progression of the value flow to identify some milestones and signposts that can help us evaluate production from the standpoint of the value relationship. Then, using this information, we can see how this conception overall supports the holographic nature of the positions, jobs, and functions in the production process.

The production process we envision is not a special or new way of moving an idea along through stages toward completion in a product or service. And the names of the departmental groups involved—R&D, operations, marketing, sales, and so on—may not change. Our endeavor here is to see each of these steps from a different perspective. Here, they are evaluated on the basis of the extent to which, and the effectiveness with which, they engage customer concerns that have the potential to create value.

So what we are talking about here is a progression through different qualities of attention and action, based on what the value relationship requires, that each worker and/or manager applies in the course of his or her work. We all know that when we undertake any activity, we have to vary the quality and kind of attention we apply, depending on where in the process we are.

When a baseball player is waiting on deck, about to hit, he is concentrating in a certain way. He may concentrate his attention on the pitcher's delivery point and try to get a sense of the timing intervals between the windup and when the ball crosses the plate. The attention is mostly a mental exercise. When he steps up to the plate, however, a different kind of attention and action is called for—one of intense concentration on the ball, a nearly unconscious response when the pitch is on the way that explodes in a culminating swing at the ball.

Similarly, people's attention, concentration, and actions are focused differently at different stages of the production process. We distinguish three "moments"—identifiably different kinds of attention and actions—in the flow of value: *discernment, operational production*, and *transactional production*. In the final analysis, examining how value flows through the production process assesses the business's ability to marshal talents, resources, and concentration on a meaningful response to its relationship.

Holographic Production Strategy

Before we go into a detailed description of these models of attention in the value process, we need to explain a bit more about how they accord with our holographic principles we have taken such care to enumerate.

In sum, we can say that each position or job has a singular role or place in the process as a whole, but each position also participates in the value relationship of the business as a whole. We saw this as the "redundancy" aspect of holographic organizations previously. Here we can be more specific. In a holographic organization, a lathe operator does not only shape the piece of metal or wood according to tightly predefined specifications; he also has an appreciation for how this piece contributes to the overall quality of the finished product, what each micrometer of tolerance means in terms of performance. The operator is aware of the whole process of production and is able to contribute to others' understanding and to the overall effectiveness of the production process.

This means that production is not considered to move through the organization in a straight line, as it does in classical production strategies. Instead, it moves in a helixlike pattern, with epicycles at each station along the way. The epicycles at each station represent the fact that each participant is involved in all three moments—discernment, operational production, and transactional production—while in the process of performing each specialized task. In this way, the business's total value relationship is replicated in each person and each stage in the process (see Figure 13.1).

Productivity takes on quite a different meaning when judged by each person's contribution to the flow of value through the organization. The productivity question is no longer, Is this person performing up to the time per unit standard? In the context of a value flow, the question is, Is this person contributing to the company's value relationship by performing his or her function to the full potential required?

There are many differences we could point to between production viewed as a linear progression of product making versus the epicyclic process of advancing the flow of value through the organization. One difference that is particularly instructive, however, is that at each step of the production process a person independently assesses the methods and outcomes of his or her contribution.

The lathe operator, for example, is not only concerned with how fast a piece is turned and the tolerances achieved in that time. He can also raise the further questions: Is this the best way to make this piece? Does this specified tolerance give the results that the standard for quality requires? Are these the right materials to use for this part? Do I have the equipment and support to do the job right?

As mentioned earlier, Gareth Morgan calls this kind of process "double loop learning."[1] Single loop learning has three steps: (1) "sensing, scanning, monitoring the environment," (2) comparison of this information

Figure 13.1
Classical Versus Value-Based Views of the Production Process

CLASSICAL PRODUCTION SEQUENCE
FOR PRODUCT DEVELOPMENT

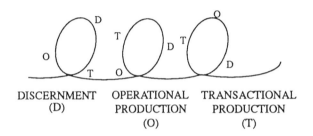

DISCERNMENT   OPERATIONAL   TRANSACTIONAL
(D)   PRODUCTION   PRODUCTION
                (O)   (T)

EPICYCLIC VALUE FLOW
THROUGH PRODUCTION

Note: Each epicycle contains the moments of discernment,
operational production, and transactional production.

against operating norms, and (3) the process of initiating appropriate
action. In our example, this would mean the operator would get his
orders; compare them to requirements, standards, output rates, and
defect standards he has known in the past; and then get to work.

Double loop learning adds an additional loop to step two. In addition
to comparing the information gathered in step one to operating norms,
workers, such as the lathe operator, also add the second loop, questioning
whether these operating norms are appropriate by asking more probing
and challenging kinds of questions. Any organization, in order to adapt
to its environment, has to realize whether or not, and/or when, it is time
to change its norms, expectations, and habits of perception, conception,
and action. The second loop encourages each and every part of the
organization to participate in determining what is important in its relationships with its customers (see Figure 13.2).

Classical strategies use single loop learning processes. They have decided in advance what criteria are appropriate for determining the suc-

Figure 13.2
Single Loop Versus Double Loop Learning

SINGLE LOOP LEARNING

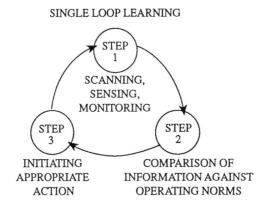

DOUBLE LOOP LEARNING

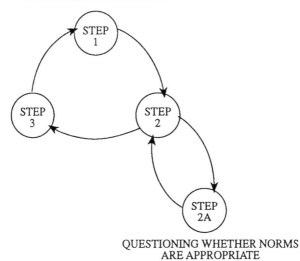

Source: From Morgan, *Images of Organization*, p. 88.

cess of their actions—and thus what in the relationships the business
undertakes it thinks is important to assess, measure, and use for further
decision making. Capital-based organization strategy sets up its rate of
return on equity as a standard and norm of performance, and that is
the end of discussion. All actions must support and contribute to this

one goal. Management-based strategy uses market-oriented criteria such as market share as their standard, which are likewise inviolately final.

The value flow ensures that there is a second loop in two ways. First, each step in the process has its discernment phase. As we shall see, this means each step in the process begins with an assessment of what opportunities a value relationship presents and what in the production process needs to be improved and/or corrected.

Second, each step in the value flow views the actions involved as being produced by those involved in the process. Operational production is a process of producing the operation procedures, standards, and practices by means of which a product is made or service is delivered. Transactional production, similarly, is the process of devising opportunities and methods for continued customer contact after the product is made or service designed. Each person, at each step in the process, is accountable for what Robert Burgelman has called "autonomous strategic behavior."[2] Each person is responsible for offering observations and initiatives that produce the organization's production capabilities.

DISCERNMENT

Discernment moves production beyond the quantifiable and even beyond the predictable into the realm of the possible, the probable, and the projected. The basic question that gives rise to discernment is, How is my business's product-enabled activity affecting people's lives? From this, other questions ensue: What qualities do people expect from the interactions? Are they getting it? What other interactions, technologies, or services does this interaction connect with? Are there opportunities there? Are there opportunities to improve or differentiate the product based on these interactions?

Any business spends a great deal of time and resources on the management-driven functions of marketing, forecasting, and other anticipatory activities. Generally, these actions take the form of tracking sales in units and dollars and monitoring market share. They are also used to closely examine competing products by "reverse engineering," or systematically disassembling them to see how they are made. Some companies research their competitors to anticipate the direction their decisions may take. All of these efforts represent important efforts to keep current with how problems and opportunities are being addressed, and they provide important benchmarks for self-assessment. But they are largely defensive. They are used to assess how existing products, or known product development, will affect their own plans.

Discernment, in contrast, examines how the value relationship fulfills and resolves expectations and demands for the buyer and also what it *does not* resolve. It uncovers opportunities for creating new requirements, demands, and expectations. In discernment, people survey the living value relationship to which the business is dedicated—its customers' activities as well as its own actions—for openings that indicate a basis for another or a new interaction, some innovation, modification, or product improvement.

The best source of this information is direct, person-to-person contact with customers. As Andrew Van de Ven expresses it, interaction with customers

> will increase the likelihood that the action threshold of organizational participants will be triggered and will stimulate them to pay attention to changing environmental conditions or customer needs. In general we would expect that direct personal confrontations with problem sources are needed to reach the threshold of concern and appreciation required to motivate people to act.[3]

Rosabeth Moss Kanter points out that "three-fourths of a set of 500 important individual innovations owed their origins to user suggestions and even user interventions." Users, or customers, generated 81 percent of ideas for scientific instruments and 60 percent of ideas for process machinery.[4]

In the terms of our definition of value, customer contact taps into the energies of prospect, imagination, and desire, which is where the value relationship begins. Quantitative market research ascertains how people are projecting the use of a product and whether or not it contains the right features, price, and manner of distribution that makes sense to people. Market share and sales reports give adequate readings of whether or not it meets criteria for procurement, if it is accessible and intelligible in use, and if it passes the crucial test of favorable reconsideration.

But these reports only provide information on the later procurement stages of the value process. They do not derive from what occurs in the earlier generative and formative stages of the process—prospection and projection—when the potential buyer envisions a resolution to her situation and how she is factoring the enablement in her life-style. Only by tapping into the prospection and projection phases of the value experience can new dimensions open up as to possible business responses to the value relationship.

One company that exemplifies the power of discernment as a spur to production is Sony. Sony eschews the standard kinds of marketing research. Rather than look at competition in the consumer electronics industry as a matter of combining price with technology, it looked at the way people used to hear music or watch television programs and thought long and hard about what that activity entailed.[5] From this consideration of the experience of enjoying sound and image came the ideas for the

Walkman, the Watchman, and the compact disk player—three innovations that have reshaped consumer electronics. From there, further refinements have been made in making the instruments smaller, lighter, and longer playing.

These insights led to other kinds of decisions that ripple all the way through the production process. Sony now developed the technologies that support its ability to respond to the value relation. Sony, for instance, is now a leader in producing microprocessors—a major component of its products—and sells them to other computer makers such as Apple as well.

This is the creative aspect of discernment. But discernment also acts as the "reality check" for other sources of innovation-generating activities used by a business. As we saw in chapter 6, when we discussed the concept of "increasing returns," too many forces are at work in any market to rest assured that technological correctness, or marketing muscle, for that matter, will make a product a success. John Hendry, for example, has found that an effective way to increase the effectiveness of R&D is to increase these people's contact and interaction with sales and marketing people. These "dynamic networks," of mixed skills and orientation, are able to bring to bear all the information and experience that are available in the product development process.[6]

Sony's own experience with the failure of its Betamax video system—superior by far in terms of technology to the VHS format—demonstrates what can happen if discernment is too narrow, is driven by technology only, or is incompletely considered. One can only wonder what information was missing in Coca-Cola's misfire with its New Coke. Coke tried to emulate PepsiCola's sweeter beverage, which was garnering sales among young people, but completely misread the original product's status with its existing customers. New Coke failed.

Upper management must lead the way in fostering customer contact and instilling discernment as a core principle of production. If the boss shows that this is important, everyone will realize that dealing with customers, and valuing the departments and personnel who do this every day, is a part of everyone's job.

Of course, everyone in the company cannot be involved with every customer. But meaningful contacts can be maintained with the business's most difficult customers by means of user groups, consultants, and direct-service personnel. Motorola, for instance, assigns senior managers to act as "champions" for particular customers, ensuring that the customer's voice will be heard throughout the organization. Harley-Davidson's vice president spends weekends out riding with his customers. This activity helped turn the company away from the brink of extinction in the early eighties to being once again the preeminent American motorcycle company.

OPERATIONAL PRODUCTION

Production that begins with discernment accepts the terms, requirements, and conditions of the business's value relationships, not as they are now but as they are envisioned by its customers. When production begins, everyone in the organization is facing a world of possibilities. Translating discernment into tasks, as Van de Ven describes it, is a process of both "harvesting good ideas" and providing a "vehicle for otherwise disconnected or competitive individuals and stakeholders to come together and contribute their unique frames of reference to the innovation process."[7]

More than a process of maintaining operations, operational production is a process of producing the framework that transforms a business's operations into a process capable of creating value. Kanter cites six kinds of ideas that are more likely to attract support and be translated into tasks: *trialable*, ideas that can be worked out in demonstration projects; *divisible*, ideas that can be broken up into steps or phases for gradual experimentation, testing, and evaluation; *consistent with sunk costs*, ideas that build on prior commitments that the company has already made; *concrete and tangible*, ideas that are easily understandable and translate easily into actions; *congruent*, ideas that fit with current and compelling organizational directions; and ideas that have *publicity value*.[8]

In bringing new ideas to fruition, human knowledge takes on a preeminent role over mere technology. As Ramchandran Jaikuman points out, it is not a matter of investing in new equipment "but how the equipment is used that is important. Success comes from achieving continuous process improvement through organizational learning and experimentation." "Intellectual assets," as he calls them, become the flexible interface between incremental change and existing production capability and structure.[9] Operational production is the process of maintaining a balance between change or the push for new ideas and continuity with the company's mission and resource capabilities.

This is not a strictly intellectual process of putting goals in one column and decisions in another column opposite them. In production, actions are being undertaken that to a greater or lesser degree have not yet been undertaken by anyone, creating a community of equals in dealing with the new. Operational production thus merges with organizational strategy in that the aim of production is to ensure that the organization is in a position to implement the changes it must make.

Kanter has studied some of the important factors in implementing "learning to learn" strategies on the operational level. Adapting her observations to our value-based operational level. Adapting her observations to our value-based outlook, we can clearly see some of the important factors that contribute to the kind of value-based production strategy about which we are talking.

• *Kaleidoscopic thinking.* This refers to the ability of an organization to "construct new ways" to address new needs. "Cross fertilization" is another way she expresses this idea that organizations encourage contact and open communications between people with widely divergent ideas or cross-disciplinary ideas.

• *Intersecting territories.* Akin to the holographic conception of "requisite variety," this idea refers to the organization's ability to sustain and achieve results even when it exhibits a high degree of complexity. The organizations, such as Sony or other technology organizations we have already referred to, require many sources of information, many different functions, talents, and kinds of expertise. In the successful companies, people have the freedom to explore the many options and resources their organizations provide.

• *Broad jobs.* People's jobs are not defined by identification with a task but are related to solving problems. They are not defined in terms of a place in the routine or standard operating procedure but relationally, in terms of what they contribute to the company's value relationship. And the production process depends on their ability to respond to situations quickly, creatively, without a lot of intervening and energy-sapping formality.

• *Integration.* This means that people are not segmented and departmentalized from each other. In a low-wall culture, people can connect and intersect in ways appropriate to solve problems. Once an innovation is undertaken, the organization allows it to proceed and encourages the group's coalescing and autonomy.[10]

In operational production, each member in the organization participates in redirecting and reapplying resources according to the requirements and challenges at hand. Production yields not only a product but an organization that responds to the people in it. According to Robert Hayes, Japan spends 40 percent of its R&D budget on improving equipment and processes.[11] In our own country, Motorola has a policy that each employee is expected to participate in forty hours of education and training per year, or a minimum 2 percent of each employee's time. In 1989, it spent $1.8 billion or 19 percent of revenues on R&D, training, and capital improvements. In 1990, when other companies were cutting back on R&D as a percentage of sales, owing to the recession, Motorola increased its ratio.[12]

Of course, it is understood that production is always a process of providing enablements where quality must be achieved under the demands of tight cost parameters, controls, and close monitoring, which are absolutely necessary. Nevertheless, when viewed from the perspective of value strategy, performance efficiency does not necessarily lead to production effectiveness. Operational effectiveness requires that each person contribute to the company's essential relationship to its customers to the maximum potential called for by the position and its function.

An example of how this works was reported recently in the *New York Times*.[13] In 1987, Nelson Metal Products Corporation, a $68 million manufacturing company, was about to be dropped as a supplier to Ford Motor Company and General Motors. The automakers were dissatisfied with Nelson's defect ratio of twenty-five hundred parts per million. In its efforts to remedy the situation and save the company, Nelson achieved production effectiveness by ensuring that the right voices and opinions were heard on the critical issues. Nelson carefully instituted a process in which each person in each step of production was queried as to what problems were encountered; each person queried was responsible for coming up with suggestions to make improvements. As a result of this process, Nelson and its employees turned the company around.

One department increased production of a part from 80 to 140 per hour. The reason this was possible was that the head of the group was recruited from a nonproduction department and was not invested in a particular solution. He made sure many voices were heard, not just the foreman's, who would have pushed his idea over against others. In other situations, corporate officers led teams, ensuring that each participant prepared for the meeting and offered meaningful suggestions with the expectation that something might come of the suggestion. Now the company is a highly respected supplier, with a defect ratio of fewer than 10 parts per million.

To accomplish effectiveness, controls on production from moment to moment are often loosened. Federal Express Corporation, the express delivery company, tried conventional methods for getting more efficiency out of their operators. They limited each call to 140 seconds and monitored the calls, measuring the time it took its twenty-five hundred customer-service agents to handle a problem. Beating the clock constituted 50 percent of an agent's review. The reps complained that the time limits caused too much stress and forced them to cut off customers before their questions were answered.

In response, the company relaxed monitoring calls for time (a supervisor now monitors a random call two times a year) and let the operators talk to customers more loosely. The conversations stayed short anyway—

actually dropped to 135 seconds—and they often led to opportunities for the operators to inform customers of additional services or money-saving enhancements.[14]

Bell Canada tried the same strategy, and as a result their productivity increased 70 percent. At issue within the group is not only the perfunctory completion of the production step but the consciousness of this function contributing to the quality of a buyer's ongoing interactions with this product.[15]

Operational production adopts a strategic orientation to production that aims to improve the process, not just the output. Decision makers, concerned about the quality of operational production, focus not just on monitoring the costs of day-to-day operations; they also choose projects that develop the business's intellectual and physical assets. Concentration on "system design and organization" of highly skilled generalists replaces Tayloresque sweat-of-the-brow specialization.

Operations are usually done in-house, where contact with the customer is most easily lost amid concerns for cost per unit, productivity in units per hour or per position, and other internally motivated, cost-side issues. The purpose of looking at operations as a phase in a flow of value is to correct this bias. Operational production takes the customers' point of view, their standards of quality and expectations for the enablement, and translates these into commitment and focus at each position. Each employee understands and is committed to some aspect of the business's value relationship.

Motorola's quality program emphasized just this point. In a briefing document for executives who were being trained in the "Six Sigma" Quality Program,[16] each person was trained to identify six steps that defined his or her manufacturing task:

1. Identify the product you create or the service you provide.
2. Identify the customer(s) for your product or service and determine what they consider important.
3. Identify your needs (to provide product/service so that it satisfies the customer).
4. Define the process for doing the work.
5. Mistake-proof the process and eliminate wasted effort.
6. Ensure continuous improvement by measuring, analyzing, and controlling the improved process.

This policy clearly articulates the ideas we have grouped under *operational production*. It keeps everyone's focus on generating the kinds of operations that are defined by customer requirements. In Motorola's case, one result from orienting its policies and evaluation criteria toward value-based principles was reducing the number of parts in its cellular phone to four hundred, only 12 percent of the number of parts it had in its 1978 model. Using a combination of workers and robots, those parts are now assembled in two hours instead of the forty hours required in 1985.[17]

TRANSACTIONAL PRODUCTION

Production creates value by solidifying a cycle of expectation, satisfaction, and renewed expectation for the products buyers willingly incorporate into their life-style as enablements. Production must continue into the phase of the value-creating process when the product already exists—and even beyond, to when it has been sold and is being used. This is an obvious conclusion in the case of services. But even when it comes to products, it must be remembered that at the point of completed manufacturing no value has as yet been created. Transactional production is the process of performing *education* in the proper sense of the term: leading the buyer out of one way of doing things and into another.

Transactional production occurs in four stages: integration, communication, selling, and service.

Integration

A product—or in some cases, the enablement itself—must compete for attention and incorporation into buyer's daily lives at work and at home, or it must establish its own category of activity as part of their lives. As we saw earlier, there are so many factors at work in determining whether or not a product will become successful, that it is nearly impossible for the business's decision makers, in most cases, to predict what will happen once the product reaches the market.

What the business itself can shape to a much greater extent is the level of integration its product category is able to achieve in the lives of buyers. That is, the decision makers can't know for sure if their product will sell, but they can be sure that every possible effort is made to establish the good reputation of the company and achieve the widest possible knowledge and appreciation of those efforts to meet some requirement of potential buyers.

As we saw earlier, integration is the process of establishing the conditions that support the enablement as a feasible alternative for resolving buyers' requirements. To undertake integration successfully requires efforts that go far beyond inventing a product or service and carrying out an introduction with a lot of hoopla, slick packaging, and trendy advertising.

It even means more than meeting people's needs. Many products for which there is a need fail because there is no "market." That is, people do not as yet envision the enablement as a whole or as a complete set of interrelated products and activities that resolve situations with desirable outcomes. As an example, Osborne's early portable computer was the right idea and met a need. But because all the necessary technologies (flat panel displays, compact memory disks, and large capacity memory) were not in place and because there was insufficient applications software available, this necessary product, at that time, did not have a market. By not having sufficient integrating support, it did not provide people with a new way to engage their world in a significant way. It was successful as a novelty among computer enthusiasts, but as a viable enablement, it failed.

Now, with all these and other technological features in place, the laptop computer is the leading edge of retail computer sales, accounting for 35 percent of all personal computers sold in the United States in 1990. In 1990, 832,000 were sold. By 1992, annual sales are expected to top 1.8 million.[18]

A business's ability to establish its product also depends on there being a concrete delivery system, developed to the point where it fits the expectations and style of interaction of the enablement involved.

Communication

Before integration can be completed, the business must properly and meaningfully communicate with its stakeholders (stockholders, customers, neighbors, suppliers, and competitors) about the role and significance of the enablement. This aspect of production is the process of portraying and expressing all the insights into those situations disclosed in discernment. This portrayal of the product points beyond the entity's mere utility, its features, and benefits, to the role and place it has in the buyer's life.

Communication entails a precisely focused effort to foster comprehension of the enablement within the lives of the buyers. The business becomes the advocate of the way its enablement resolves a particular situation, communicating to its customers both the image of the outcome and the salient features of the product that make the resolution possible. The act of communication presents the concept of the enablement in a way that links up with the buyers' own world of images, expectations and requirements. Pricing, merchandising, packaging, and service all reflect what is known and understood about buyers' requirements for entering into a value relationship.

Selling

Now the product must be shown to accord with each buyer's specific projections and requirements. This is no easy process. Just because a buyer envisions using an enablement in general by no means entails or necessitates the purchase of a particular product. Because a buyer wants a car does not mean she will buy a Chevy. To bridge that gap, the seller must fully understand what the buyer is projecting for this enablement, must devise a means to ferret that information out, and must then translate the product's actual characteristics and capabilities into that frame.

Selling establishes the business's most individualized or microeconomic relation with buyers. Selling proactively guides buyers' transactions with the enablement through the process of appropriation and incorporation/ use. On an individual basis, at its best, selling helps the buyer comprehend the business's interpretation of the enablement in its living context. It puts the interpretation as reflected in the product in the best light and then cultivates the buyer's acceptance of that vision. The seller strives to form a bridge between two mind-sets. On the one hand, the business has developed its conception of the enablement and has refined it throughout all the preceding phases of production. The buyer, on the other hand, knows the personal conditions to which the enablement is actually and concretely being applied. If both parties remain fixed in their respective positions, nothing will happen. No sale will be made. The selling process in its highest form is actually the process of negotiating mutual *rapprochement* that accommodates both parties' requirements. An agreement or sale incorporates the conclusions of the negotiated changes into a comprehensible and developing relationship.

One of the reasons Motorola's computer chip business has been successful in establishing a dominant position in Japan is due to what the Japanese call its *netsui*, or "passion." According to Nobuhiko Shinoda, then a section chief and now assistant general manager with Canon, he chose Motorola as the supplier of a key component of its new cameras over three Japanese competitors because he says, "From the first time we talked, they let me know how much we mattered to them." Motorola then went on to invent several other key components for Canon.

Again, as we have said before, it is also crucial that everyone be committed to the whole process of the value flow. In this case, "what really impressed Shinoda was the openness of senior Motorola executives. 'Several times,' he says, 'I'd suddenly need to talk to the guy who makes decisions in Phoenix.' He invariably was put right through to a vice-president. For a mere section chief, he adds, 'no Japanese company would do that.' "[19]

Service

At its best, service is an extension of the quality-producing aspects of production. The importance of service as a component of production emerges clearly when we remember that no value has been created until the buyer decides to incorporate this product or service into the everyday assumed and anticipated patterns of daily work and private life.

Service thus includes all aspects of production that take place after customers have the product in their hands. It encompasses all actions that ensure, or at least invite, a continued relationship between the business and its customers.

Service treats what Theodore Levitt calls the "intangibles" of products or services.[20] While his concern is how to market these intangible qualities of a business's offerings, ours is how to ensure that they are conceived as an integral part of the production process. Commonly, when a product or service is presented to a customer, the way it is supposed to deliver value is expressed in terms of "benefits." There are "product benefits," or ways that the product enables the buyer to achieve his or her goals, and there are "system" or "company benefits," ways that the company's specific policies aid and support the product or service (warranties, network of dealers or service agents, etc.).

The service component of transactional production composes an additional level of benefits we call "interactive benefits," benefits that arise from the business actively pursuing contact with customers while its product or service is in use. Interactive benefits appeal to the fact that customers use products because they have an emotional stake in the activity. They have requirements they want resolved; they have a lack, deficit, or unfulfilled state of affairs that they want to move out of. Service responds to these sensitivities. It produces interactive benefits that give buyers comfort, security, and assurance of supply and constancy with regard to the interactions the enablement entails.

If there are aspects of the business's relationship to the customer that need to be completed, or accompaniments to the prime offering that need to be in place for the buyer's interactions to succeed, they had well better be in place. Computer companies realize this keenly. No matter how good the basic machine is, a way must be found to ensure a plentiful supply and variety of software as well as ready and easily accessible assistance for users.

Dell Computer, a mail-order computer maker regarded as an upstart in 1990, was rated as the most dependable provider of service in a J. D. Power survey that year. Dell instituted "direct relationship marketing" in which, as its founder Michael S. Dell says, "we take direct responsibility for the complete satisfaction of each and every customer." Dell says 91 percent of problems are handled on the phone by a staff of 150 technicians. But for those problems that cannot be solved on the phone, Dell offers next-day, on-site service. Analysts expect the company to earn $43 million on sales of $750 million in fiscal 1992.[21]

In the case of service businesses, no matter how good and competent the personnel performance may be, in-progress communications, timely updates, and forecasts of upcoming steps in the process are all crucial to creating value.

Service completes both the cycle of the value process and the production as well. It encourages customers, by every means at the company's disposal, to incorporate the product into their lives and to anticipate the experience and capabilities it makes possible. Paying attention to the experience of buyers with the product demonstrates the business's commitment to a value-creating process and relationship. Nothing happens without it.

NOTES

1. Gareth Morgan, *Images of Organization* (Newbury Park, Calif.: Sage, 1986), pp. 87–90.

2. Robert A. Burgelman, "Corporate Entrepreneurship and Strategic Management: Insight from a Process Study," *Management Science* 29, no. 12 (December 1983): 1361.

3. Andrew H. Van de Ven, "Central Problems in the Management of Innovation," *Management Science* 32, no. 5 (May 1986): 596.

4. Rosabeth Moss Kanter, "When a Thousand Flowers Bloom: Structural, Collective and Social Conditions for Innovation in Organization," in *Research in Organizational Behavior*, vol. 10, Barry M. Staw and L. L. Cummings, eds. (Greenwich, Conn.: JAI Press, 1988), p. 174.

5. David E. Sanger, "Sonys' Norio Ohga: Building Smaller, Buying Bigger," *New York Times Magazine*, February 18, 1990, p. 22.

6. John Hendry, "Barriers to Excellence and the Politics of Innovation," *Journal of General Management* 15, no. 2 (Winter 1989): 26.

7. Van de Ven, "Central Problems in the Management of Innovation," p. 593.

8. Kanter, "When a Thousand Flowers Bloom," pp. 185–186.

9. Ramchandran Jaikuman, "Post Industrial Manufacturing," *Harvard Business Review*, November–December 1986, p. 70.

10. Kanter, "When a Thousand Flowers Bloom," pp. 175–184.

11. Robert H. Hayes, "Why Japanese Factories Work," *Harvard Business Review*, July–August 1981, p. 64.

12. "The Rival the Japanese Respect," *Business Week*, November 13, 1989, p. 109.

13. "A Revival of the Quality Circle," *New York Times*, May 26, 1991, sec. 3, p. 23.

14. "Quality Is Becoming Job One in the Office Too," *Business Week*, April 29, 1991, p. 56.

15. Ibid.

16. From an internally produced training manual obtained at a seminar.

17. "The Rival the Japanese Respect," p. 118.

18. "Laptops: The Machines Are Tiny, the Potential Is Huge," *Business Week*, March 18, 1991, p. 119.

19. "The Rival the Japanese Respect," p. 118.

20. Theodore Levitt, *The Marketing Imagination* (New York: Free Press, 1986), pp. 101–103.

21. "PC Slump? What PC Slump?" *Business Week*, July 1, 1991, p. 67.

14

Value Relationships at Work: Co-Involvement

Since a system of production that meets the demands of its value relationships is not constrained within a rigidly hierarchical, top-down structure, organizational change becomes a fact of life. Instead of being a "rational" workplace, where production moves along according to an established routine, a business always seems to be on the verge of (if not in the midst of) turmoil, conflict, and confusion. Rather than filling in positions with tightly prescribed parameters, workers in these businesses have to continually reshape their roles, learn new activities, and form new relationships with their coworkers. Instead of these businesses being places where jobs are dispassionately carried out with detachment, they are places where jobs are filled with emotional content—anxiety, excitement, commitment, and intensity.

How can decision makers organize production and manage the work under these circumstances? As is often the case, the answer is actually contained in the problem. The fact that a business is operating within ongoing value relationships means that what the organization does—the products and services it produces—has significance for its customers. This fact of business life is an open invitation to involvement and commitment on the part of everyone involved in the production process. The aim of value production strategy, therefore, is to get people to accept that invitation and transform it into initiative.

CLASSICAL MODELS OF WORK RELATIONSHIPS

In classical formulations of work relationships, managers encourage workers or "subordinates" to perform well by using incentives. They mark out a path along which subordinates will attain the kinds of rewards that are equal to, or are compensatory for, the work they have performed for the business. This is called the *path-goal model* of managing and motivating workers.

In fact, the correlation between performance and satisfaction in the work relationship is itself a problem. It cannot be statistically determined whether promised satisfaction by means of compensation induces better performance or whether high levels of performance lead to increased satisfaction. According to Edward Lawler and Lyman Porter, on the one hand, the connection between performance and satisfaction is not made by large numbers of respondents in surveys; so the connection itself is suspect.[1] On the other hand, however, it is a factor that a fraction of respondents in every survey do mention, so the correlation does have some validity, according to these authors.

From our perspective, the path-goal model works fairly well as long as the outcome of production and the rate of return on investment are predictable within an acceptable range. The manager can promise each worker that high performance will lead to rewards because market share and profits can be predicted. But what happens if outcomes cannot be predicted, and rewards for hard work cannot be promised, as is certainly the case in today's world? There are too many variables and factors at work, such as those we described in connection with increasing returns, to make such guarantees.

Since ambiguity, uncertainty, and some risk are introduced throughout the process, tasks cannot be overlaid onto a structure, promises cannot be pegged to anticipated outcomes, and satisfaction of personal needs cannot be promised. When the "goal" portion of the path-goal formulation breaks down, the promise of satisfaction also breaks down. How does the manager motivate in that case?

If, according to classical models, the system of predictable rewards can't lead the way out of the morass, and can't supply the motivation necessary to spur performance, then the organization must need a different kind of person in the key management position, one we call the "leader." The leader as described by Abraham Zaleznik fits the picture we have in mind:

While ensuring the competence, control and the balance of power relations among groups with the potential for rivalry, managerial leadership unfortunately does not necessarily ensure imagination, creativity or ethical behavior in guiding the destinies of corporate enterprises.[2]

The leader alters the satisfaction-performance equation by displacing the workers' needs for pay, status, or other organizationally satisfied requirements with the single need to please the leader. For the subordinate, pleasing the leader, despite the long hours, the low pay, the spartan working conditions, is the satisfaction.

The classical manager and leader differ from one another on very basic personal, stylistic, and even philosophical levels. Among those differences, Zaleznik points to these:

- The managers we are accustomed to seeing in classical organizations adopt impersonal, if not passive, attitudes toward goals. The goals arise out of necessities rather than desires. Leaders, on the other hand, adopt a personal and active attitude toward goals, alter moods, evoke images and expectations, and change the way people think about what is desirable, possible, and necessary.

- These managers view work as an enabling process that they help along by all the means we have characterized in the path-goal model. "Machiavelli wrote for managers and not necessarily for leaders," says Zaleznik. Leaders, on the other hand, develop fresh approaches to problems, open old issues to new options. They seek out high-risk situations.

- Classical managers work with people according to the role they play in a sequence of events or in a decision-making process, keeping this moving along smoothly and efficiently, at the minimal emotional cost. Leaders relate in more intuitive and empathetic ways. They attract strong feelings of identity and difference, engender turbulence, intensity, and disorder.

- Classical managers have a strong sense of belonging to groups, or institutions, and invest a lot of energy in creating harmony in the group. Leaders are "twice born," as Zaleznik says. "They may work in organizations, but they never belong to them. Their sense of who they are does not depend on memberships, work roles or other social indicators of identity."[3]

Leaders appear to have all the qualities necessary to meet the kinds of challenges turnover and changing customer requirements demand. But in reality, this leadership approach only delays the problems and the inevitable confrontation with their consequences. The core defect of this approach, as we have discussed, is that it constricts decision making within a small, elite, supposedly all-knowing group of people in the organization.

In the classical model, whether the person is considered to be a leader or a manager, only he (and it is usually a man) wears the mantle of logic, vision, and power. Only those in the designated inner group are vested with decision-making prerogative and strategy-formulating power. The main difference between the leader and the manager is that the classical manager uses a logical, procedural rationale to justify his actions, whereas the leader relies on the force of his personality or the power of well-articulated images and ideas to evoke responses from others.

It is easy to see why a managed company might turn to a leader in times of stress and crisis, as Chrysler Corporation did in turning over the reigns to Lee Iacocca, who certainly qualifies as a successful leader in the classical mold. But, we must ask, while leaders of this type can take an organization out of the wilderness, can this personality be consistently constructive enough in the situation we address, where complex change and turnover are incessant and the normal state of affairs? Neither Steve Jobs nor Lee Iacocca has been able to do that. Steve Jobs was relieved of his position in the company he founded, and Chrysler Corporation suffered from numerous defections among the corporate hierarchy.

The classical manager many indeed prove unequal to the task, but the leader will burn out everyone in his path, including himself. Neither offers a prescription for the long haul. Clearly, another vision and managerial prototype must be developed.

CO-INVOLVEMENT

Replacing both the path-goal and leadership models is the value-based concept I call *co-involvement*. Going beyond cooperation wherein people *do things* together to produce a result, co-involvement fosters situations in which people combine ideas, initiative, interest and energy on multiple levels to create something new (see Figure 14.1).

The principal characteristic of co-involvement is that the management and/or leadership function is diffused throughout the group and is distributed among people according to the skills, interests, and personalities they offer to the group. Neither disciplinarian supervisors nor inspirational leaders drive subordinates in lockstep with their conclusions. Rather, all participants in production engage in a process of internalizing and learning in action. Leadership emerges out of the work process and within the context of ongoing dialogue and sharing with "associates" (as workers are now called in many organizations that have adopted this mode of production).

Participants formulate their own responses to the business's value relationship. All parties are involved in the evolution—indeed, the evocation—of the idea into a shared process of fulfillment, motivation, and action. Leadership emerges out of the group process of assimilating the demand of the value relationship into the real-life situation in which the

Figure 14.1
Classical Versus Co-Involvement Models of Work Relationships

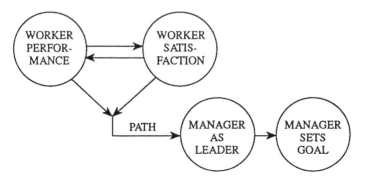

CLASSICAL PATH/GOAL MODEL

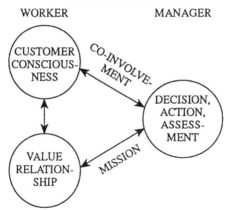

CO-INVOLVEMENT MODEL

business finds itself. Management's role in comparison to classical models is turned inside out. It becomes one of keeping the directed value flow intact as it progresses back and forth between the business's collective definition of its essential value relationship and the participant's individual conception of it.

Motivation

The idea that work must be onerous and alienating is a holdover from the days when, as Robert Hayes says, our system "deskilled" its workers, when managers funneled workers' energies to tending machines.[4] At the beginning of this century, Émile Durkheim noted that with the decline of the supporting institutions of the church and family, work settings had the potential of being places of support and fulfillment. That may have been asking too much, but work can be a positive experience.

When there are neither guarantees of outcome nor charismatic leaders to entice performance, motivation must take the form of a *commitment* on the worker's part to all aspects of the business's value relationship. Each participant voluntarily shapes his or her actions to the parameters of the value relationship. This voluntarily chosen commitment creates an internalized focal point that is capable of fully commanding all the energy and attention required to successfully address the challenge presented by the discerned opening and the operational and transactional actions that follow.

That value relationship becomes an *imperative* on a personal level: a freely adopted dedication of personal time, resources, thought, sweat, feeling, and energy in order to sustain or to bring about a value relationship. The relationship is both personally envisioned and unambiguously adopted as a project worthy of personal concentration and attention.

One psychological or motivational model that is frequently cited in support of this kind of thinking is that of Abraham Maslow, who developed a "hierarchy of needs." His premise is that lower "deficiency" needs, such as shelter and food, have to be "filled," like empty holes, before growth needs can emerge.[5] But once those needs are met, the growth needs, such as the need for recognition, esteem, and achievement, come to the fore. Then, an even higher class of needs, that of "self-actualization," arises. Here, a person needs to define the terms of self-gratification and also needs to be involved in shaping how those terms come into being. This person is not satisfied with merely being provided for but needs to realize his or her self-defined potential. Models of satisfaction based on an individual's voluntary commitment appeal to this level of growth needs or needs for self-actualization.

The research of Frederick Herzberg in the late sixties also supports the idea that work can be stimulating and rewarding when it is properly motivated with "vertical job loading," meaning that controls were built into jobs that had with them the possibility of achievement, recognition, responsibility, advancement, and growth.[6] In other words, jobs were structured so as to integrate a wide spectrum of the higher needs Maslow alludes to. He introduced the idea that jobs must have intrinsic worth. Routine jobs that merely accomplish a task in the least amount of time with the minimum of material resources applied are deemed to be less satisfying and more likely to suffer from poor performance.

More recently, the research of Mihaly Csikszentmihalyi has shown that work can be regarded as an optimal experience by all parties involved in the process.[7] Csikszentmihalyi defines optimal experience as a "flow" in which people are fully, unself-consciously engaged in life, growing and expanding with a high degree of satisfaction. He found that 54 percent of people working at their jobs reported being in flow, and only 16 percent responded as being apathetic or bored. This compares with people doing so-called leisure activities, such as dining out, watching television, or having friends over; only 18 percent responded that they were in flow, and 52 percent said they were apathetic.[8]

This kind of self-motivating operational orientation has been achieved across many types of industries. Recent resistance to unionization in new industries as well as in facilities in traditional industries where unions had a stronghold may be an indication that employers are loading jobs with responsibility, discretion, and intrinsic worth, whereas unions are still thinking in terms of job descriptions, slots, and punch clocks.

The recent failure of the United Automobile Workers (UAW) to organize the Nissan auto plant in Smyrna, Tennessee, in 1989 is an example. Set up into small,, self-managed work teams, workers here have a degree of responsibility and autonomy in their jobs not permitted in traditional assembly lines. The union lost the vote by better than a two-to-one margin. The apparent reason was the perception that the union would represent a *loss* of autonomy and discretion in making production decisions.

At Nordstrom, an individual's initiatives in providing distinctive service to customers are encouraged, but these efforts often result in long hours and nontraditional tasks that go far beyond the usual retail job description. In a recent, hotly contested vote, Nordstrom employees voted two to one to oust the union that had raised objections to the company's expectation of individual initiative. The union's leader has now moved on. The struggle and controversy, but not the voting results, were even the subject of a *60 Minutes* segment in 1990.

In another instance, Harvard clerical workers, in 1989, authorized a union in order to ensure the quality of worker input in their job definitions, evaluation, and grievance procedures. Even though traditional issues of wages and benefits were leading factors initiating the drive to unionize, the union finally won the slim victory because it pioneered a co-involvement type of working relationship with management.

Jobs, Power, and Politics

Hierarchical organizations engender politics. Politics in organizations arise when employees believe that one can only gain satisfaction by accumulating power and that power is accumulated only by climbing the ever narrowing corporate ladder.

Since individual talents are called on to address the problems and challenges presented by the business's value relationship, there is less of a propensity to think of satisfaction as being "doled out" by management or as being channeled into narrowing paths of opportunity on the corporate power ladder. Power relationships also change dramatically from being the one-way ability to fire someone—although it is that, of course—to a two-way expectation that action will be taken.

In a co-involvement model, it is expected that persuasive skill, attention, and persistence will be applied to the task of assigning resources to meet the requirements of the value relationship. If the expectations are not met, the person (manager or team member) is removed. Power is not a force one person lords over others but a force shared with others in order to respond to the challenges at hand. The power is thus not vested in a position. The strategy is the power, and the organization is the license to use it.

In many companies, production is already organized into work groups in which co-involvement models are already in use. *Concurrent engineering, quality circles,* and *interactive decision making* are some of the names these efforts are given. This model has not been adopted because decision makers have suddenly become more "enlightened"; it is a strategic matter of survival. Challenges to the production process are too demanding and the pace of change is too fast for any one person—or even a group of homogeneous people such as a managerial brain trust. A wide range of knowledge and experience must be brought into play even to conceive of a solution, let alone to arrive at the concrete steps that will be needed to actually come out with a final product or service. Co-involvement changes the definition of a "job." Instead of being a predefined task or "slot" in the predetermined process, a job becomes what the person holding it creates by virtue of the energy, talents, and initiative brought to bear on the problem.

In this way, co-involvement attempts to break down the organizational and creative logjams that give rise to politics by opening up multiple avenues to success, recognition, and fulfillment. Realizing that may different kinds of talents and temperaments are necessary and valued within the company, decision makers have changed how compensation, recognition, and rewards are determined. Many businesses are replacing the narrowing corporate ladder path to success with multiple paths.

Some of the ideas that are being tried are lateral moves, which increase a worker's knowledge of the business, adding responsibility and autonomy to each position; pegging raises to performance rather than position; establishing "chairs" or other honored positions—with perks—for contributing in special ways to the mission; and offering overseas positions as recognition and training for the future. Other companies actually provide seed money for employees to start their own businesses in which the parent company will eventually have a major stake. Hyatt Hotel

Corporation and AT&T are two that have received attention for this practice recently.[9]

In Tracy Kidder's book, *The Soul of a New Machine*,[10] Thomas West, the leader of the group followed in the book, likens the reward system to pinball: If you win (by getting a successful product out), you get to play again; if you're successful at building this machine, you get to build another one.[11]

Stress

Co-involvement does not necessarily lead to a harmonic work process. To the contrary, one person's solution may indeed diminish or even contradict another's. There are grounds for many different solutions that generate many legitimate and hurtful conflicts. Conflict resolution emerges as one of the largest responsibilities leaders must assume. If there is no clear reading of the demands of the value relationship and no clear conception of the organization's willingness to respond to the situation, the effort is bound to fail. Experimentation, multiple directions, competition, and acting in the face of incomplete solutions are all necessary; but regardless, decisions must be made in a timely way, at appropriate milestones in the process.

Rosabeth Moss Kanter has documented and neatly categorized many of these conflicts. For example, she cites overload as a consequence of the new demands of production: People are working longer hours. In smaller businesses, fifty-two- to fifty-seven-hour workweeks are deemed normal (three more than in 1979), with 88 percent of executives in 1988 stating that they work ten or more hours per day, whereas only 44 percent did so in 1984.

Along with the longer hours goes increased intellectual and emotional absorption. With many workers now being offered wide-open vistas for exercising their talents and energies, work has a content of challenge and an aura excitement that is intrinsically attractive. Kanter also reports that with increased emotional and intellectual energy being invested in work, along with the integration of women into the workplace, more of people's emotional lives are played out in the workplace. There are more office romances, and there are increased tensions between work and family.

According to Kanter, the four leading factors that contribute to stress are the following:

1. *The communications imperative.* More hours are spent in meetings, explaining goals, and negotiating with people from whom things are needed or with whom responsibilities might overlap, and so on.

2. *The expandable activity slate and oversupply of management tasks.* This includes not only an increase in the number of people reporting to a manager but an increase in the number of projects a manager takes on. There are few standards, if any, for what is enough.

3. *A dramatic increase in the number of people who can initiate.*

4. *The exhilaration of living on the edge.*

To deal with this volatile situation, she proposes these four guidelines:

1. Delegate authority along with responsibility so that people can actually carry out what they have accepted as their goals and tasks.

2. Minimize simultaneous changes—a matter of setting and keeping to priorities so that smaller (possibly more frequently arising) matters don't put pressure on larger, more constant and important issues.

3. Emphasize simplicity over complexity. Let some tasks, procedures, programs, and roles pass out of existence. Constantly prune the operation of the unnecessary and unessential.

4. Adopt a long-range outlook on the worker's life, allowing for downtimes, when the priority of family or personal issues will be accommodated within the organization.[12]

No Shortcuts or Panacea

No one, least of all me or the writers I cite in this volume, would presume to console managers with the claim that using a co-involvement strategy will be the easy way to success. To the contrary, workers' experiences in these settings often engender nostalgia for the "good old days." And for many, they *were* good—when jobs were jobs; raises, promotions, and pensions followed good work; and you knew where you stood. I personally have noticed that in many high-tech companies, young engineers come in, fired up and ready for the fray, but by the time they reach their mid-thirties, they are tired and burned out; some are disillusioned by all the commotion and tumult.

But in my experience, both nostalgia and burnout are most likely to occur in settings where turnover-based problems, such as short product life cycles and the need for continual innovation, are handled by classically trained managers who use tenets that are appropriate to classical organizations and classical assumptions about markets, customers, and products.

In one cutting-edge, high-tech capital equipment company I worked with several years ago, the pressure for innovation was constant. The pressure came from the rapid changes and successive enhancements made to its customers' end products. To respond to the pressure, my client, a medium-sized company, with $60 million in sales and three hundred employees in the United States, Europe, and Japan when I was consulting there, initiated new and often competing projects with great energy and with ever increasing frequency. The young engineers became inured to the latest announcement of the "priority of the week."

The projects mostly failed, because, for one thing, projects were added, one on top of another, old ones rarely being put to bed. Sometimes engineers were working on two different and competing projects at the same time, under different managers. As a result, communications and administration of these layers of projects on similar or closely related subsystems became confused. I often had to spend days working with engineers to sort out the respective terminologies used in the bills of materials so that other departments down the development line could follow which project or subsystem was being referred to.

While these were stress-producing and serious problems in themselves, I believe these problems arose and that the projects ultimately failed because they were managed according to classical rubrics of productivity: maximal output, with the least cost, in the shortest amount of time. Engineers were not allowed to make mistakes. Products were thus shipped that did not quite meet the demands they were meant for, often without proper documentation and, frequently, without knowledgeable and trained field support being available.

These product-killing things happened, not because managers were incompetent or because the engineers didn't know how to do product development; they happened because everyone was under the wrong kinds of pressure. The engineers were forced to perform in ways that were inappropriate for their customers' requirements and below par for the world-class competition that was on the horizon.

In violation of the kinds of rules Kanter talks about, multiple and competing products were developed, fragmenting attention and depleting scarce resources. Engineers did not have the authority to determine what solutions were truly called for, even though many of them had detailed knowledge of the equipment involved and knew the customers for years. Decisions as to what solutions would be pursued were the province of the Marketing Department and the divisional vice presidents. The young engineers were stroked by being put at the cutting edge of technology but were also precariously placed on the precipice of performance.

Ultimately, the company failed. Once independent, with a 96 percent market share in the equipment it sold, it is now a struggling subsidiary of a large conglomerate—always rumored to be up for sale—with an insignificant market share. Only Japanese and European companies now supply this vital equipment. I am still in touch with many of the people that were involved in the company years ago. Many of those I worked most closely with have shunned the large, established high-tech company and have started new high-tech companies that they vow to keep small. Others have started technical service and consulting businesses, have gone into technical sales, or have left high tech all together.

This is not an unusual story, I am sure. But it is a sad one, and it is one that a thoroughgoing value strategy can prevent from happening in the future. However, if this kind of strategy is to work, ideas such as the value flow and co-involvement will require that close attention be paid to a new model of how to manage production. This subject is the focus of our attention in the next chapter.

NOTES

1. Edward E. Lawler, III and Lyman W. Porter, "The Effects of Performance on Job Satisfaction," *Industrial Relations* 7, no. 1 (October 1967): 20–28.

2. Abraham Zaleznik, "Managers and Leaders: Are They Different?" in *Strategic Management, Harvard Business Review Executive Book Series*, Richard G. Hamermesh, ed. (New York: John Wiley, 1983), p. 445.

3. Ibid., pp. 449–453.

4. Robert H. Hayes, "Why Japanese Factories Work" *Harvard Business Review*, July–August 1981, p. 64.

5. William E. Kilbourne, "Self-Actualization and the Consumption Process: Can You Get There from Here?" in Firat, Dholakia, and Bagozzi, eds. *Philosophical and Radical Thought in Marketing* (Lexington, Mass.: D. C. Heath, 1987), p. 221.

6. Frederick Herzberg, "One More Time: How Do You Motivate Employees?" in *The Great Writings in Management and Organizational Behavior* (Tulsa, Okla.: Petroleum, 1980).

7. Mihaly Csikszentmihalyi, *Flow: The Psychology of Optimal Experience* (New York: Harper & Row, 1990).

8. Ibid., pp. 158–159.

9. "Farewell Fast Track," *Business Week*, December 10, 1990, pp. 193–194.

10. Tracy Kidder, *The Soul of a New Machine* (Boston: Atlantic—Little, Brown, 1981).

11. See also Rosabeth Moss Kanter, *The Change Masters: Innovation and Entrepreneurship in the American Corporation* (New York: Simon & Schuster, 1983), pp. 129, 294.

12. Rosabeth Moss Kanter, *When Giants Learn to Dance* (New York: Simon & Schuster, 1989), pp. 267–297.

15

Management and Value Strategy

THE NEW MANAGEMENT REGIME

Co-involvement offers a new model of managerial interaction. Instead of manipulating the variables of performance and satisfaction, managers must elicit co-involvement by actions that husband and foster the creativity, initiative, and commitment of the members of the organization. This type of management develops in the soil of holographic organizations that have encouraged and supported the kind of autonomous strategic behavior we have talked about in previous chapters. Co-involvement invests each position with the appropriate license of managerial discretion, counteracting the tendency to concentrate those functions into designated, hierarchical positions.

Everyone in the organization is acknowledged to be able to contribute in a significant way to solutions that are meaningful and potentially profitable for the company. Managers and leaders do not suppose or even attempt to have all the answers or hold all the power. There is a distinct blurring of leader/manager versus "subordinate" status. And finally, rewards and compensation are regarded to be intrinsic to the mission and responsibilities people assume.

Extrinsic compensation—salary, status, and/or perks of any kind—are seen as necessary but are allotted on the kind of nonhierarchical basis we discussed earlier. They are also more likely to take the form of bonuses for specific accomplishments and offers of stock options to participate in the overall profitability of the company.

The managerial skills called for become those of keeping a balance between two demands. On the one hand, managers have to keep the participants open to ideas, changes, combinations of talent, energies, and personalities. On the other hand, they must encourage participants to accept the fact that their individual responses will only have "meaning," will only result in a continued process of production, if their individual solutions work in concert with others. They have to encourage full participation in and total commitment to the solutions that do emerge.

One business that has organized this way and has survived, and even thrived, in today's world is W. L. Gore & Associates, Inc., makers of the now-famous Gore-tex material used in recreational apparel as well as medical, electronic, and industrial products. The company was founded by Wilbert and Genevieve Gore because he couldn't get his idea—Teflon coating for electrical wires—marketed by his employer, Du Pont (no slouch on organizational innovation itself).

In this company, leaders can't give orders; they can only seek commitments. Each employee has a mentor who acts as a counselor and advocate. Bureaucracy is out at Gore. When plants grow to more than two hundred staffers, they are broken apart. This is reminiscent of Hewlett-Packard, which also breaks up units that grow beyond a certain benchmark. Hierarchy and status are taboo. Even the company president only reluctantly took that title. Any "perks" or status symbols are immediately dispensed with. The plant is periodically polled anonymously to ensure that the company lives up to its ideals.

In terms of a model of management and leadership, one incident at Gore clearly illustrates our point: When one employee developed a product that Gore had no way to market, he persuaded a few employees to help him out. Soon there were a few others who were interested, and soon the project team topped a dozen. "You evolve into leadership at Gore. You look behind you and you've got people following you," said the employee.

So what kind of a company is this? According to *Business Week*:

Gore isn't some little countercultural outfit, mind you....[The] company has grown into a nearly $700 million-a-year outfit, with 41 plants in six countries. Although loath to reveal profits, finance associate Shanti Mehta says Gore ranks in the top 5% of major companies in return on assets and equity. Sales have roughly tripled since 1984 and he expects they will top $1 billion within five years.[1]

ROLES, PERSONALITIES, AND NEW MANAGERIAL MODELS

To gain an insight into the kinds of personal qualifications and temperaments that are necessary to make the co-involvement model work, we turn to a brilliant short book, *Beyond Rational Management*, by Robert E. Quinn.[2] He has sorted out and named the personalities and personal qualities that are called for in the volatile environments we envision here. First, he identifies eight roles that managers have to fulfill in these kinds of environments. He divides these into "upper" and "lower" roles.

The lower roles are what managers are typically expected to do in classical organizations:

- *Monitor.* Overseeing, tracking, and measuring against goals
- *Coordinator.* Scheduling, linking, and reinforcing disparate tasks
- *Director.* Marshaling authority
- *Producer.* Accomplishing tasks with distinction

The upper roles have a different intent and orientation. In these roles, managers elicit the committed involvement of all people in the organization. I call them strategic roles because they encourage or even demand co-involvement, or "autonomous strategic behavior," in everyone in the organization. These roles are as follows:

- *Mentor.* Teaching and coaching toward independence and autonomy
- *Innovator.* Developing new, constructive solutions quickly and effectively
- *Facilitator.* Helping, assisting, connecting, and conflict resolving
- *Broker.* Wheeling and dealing on others' behalf in order to get a project going or to keep it on track

He then goes on to characterize the kinds of personality types and their orientations to the work that are effective and ineffective in those roles. These characterizations of personality types as they are reflected in the business setting are important as guides or qualitative rubrics for assessing two things. First, they help decision makers sort out the kinds of personalities they need for a particular kind of situation. A product development program that will be contentious and will stir up a lot of emotion will likely need what Quinn calls the "peaceful team builder" type of personality. A project that needs hard-nosed, no-nonsense grinding from beginning to end will need a "committed intensive" type of personality.

Second, it follows from this that after assessing what kind of personality a project needs, a decision maker can then use the kind of scheme Quinn has developed to assess the personalities of the people that are available and to create a team with the mix and balance that portend well for a project's success.

We will repeat the six personality types that Quinn cites as being effective, omitting those that are ineffective, and note some of the observations Quinn cites in his report:

1. *Conceptual producers.* These highly trained managers (78 percent with graduate educations) are seen as good at coming up with and selling new ideas. They are not detail people, but they are effective in environments where a program's coherence is not a given or easily (centrally and internally or authoritatively) maintained.

2. *Aggressive achievers.* These people score high on the lower roles (except the facilitator role) and somewhat high on the innovator role. While viewed as being highly skilled, they are not "people oriented." Interestingly, this cluster has no females! These people are probably necessary in supplying energy and concentration on detailed technical tasks, but they are by no means sufficient for coordinating or leading an entire program.

3. *Peaceful team builders.* These people, highly rated in all roles, are valued for their calming effect on people during crises. They are usually very experienced, very well educated (67 percent with graduate degrees) upper-level people. They obviously contribute stability in a volatile situation and keep the project on course.

4. *Committed intensives.* They are widely varied in the roles they play, but they all supply a well-directed intensity to the task at hand. They border on the workaholic but are just more accomplished in the roles required of managers. They are not particularly tolerant of shirkers—an invaluable asset in value-production work.

5. *Open adaptives.* These people are appreciated mostly for their contribution in the top four roles. They are obviously not the "hands-on" doers but seem to ease the political maelstroms for others on the team.

6. *Masters.* These people score unusually high ("a standard of deviation higher than the mean") on all eight roles. While individuals have weaknesses, there is no consistent weakness. Forty-six percent of this group are women.

MANAGERS AND STRATEGY

From all this, it is clear that the co-involvement model calls for selecting managers who have highly developed interactive skills, a generalist's view of the production process, and an orientation that is anything but self-centered or ego-gratifying.

We see five managerial skills that are necessary to foster co-involvement work relationships that support value-based production strategy:

1. *Choice.* This skill calls for the ability to choose from among competing options in order to achieve a compelling situation in which people can work toward their goals. This entails choices on several levels:

- Choosing the product or solution that imaginatively addresses important elements of the company's value relationships and is consistent with the company's direction and demonstrated competence and/or known success.

- Choosing the right blend of people to work together. Both some homogeneity and adequate diversity are called for: homogeneity, so that the group can form lines of communication and trust; and diversity, so that those lines of communication won't be a matter of repetition and mirror reflections, resulting in stale and repetitious perspectives.

- Choosing the right way to organize the working group. There must be a combination of autonomy and interdependence that enables each person and the group as a whole to be effective.

- Choosing the physical and material components. The site of the workplace, resources, technology, and materials must complement the demands of the project.

2. *Commitment.* This skill calls for not only being personally committed but having the ability in language, deed, and values to elicit from others the decision to commit to a project and see it through, often in the context of some sacrifice. This is possible only when everyone in the company is welcome to adopt and act on the meaning given by the company's mission.

3. *Cohesion.* This involves the ability to reinforce cohesion of the working group by listening to the ideas offered and marshaling the full range of talents that are available in the people on the team. In some quarters, this has been referred to as the "feminization" of management. And to the extent that, as Quinn cites, 46 percent of the masters are women, it is true that this might well be a factor that selects for women as managers.

But strategically speaking, holographic, value organization strategies foster those qualities in all members of the organization, regardless of gender. The purpose of a co-involvement strategy for production is to reinforce the kind of sensitivity that is able to see how a particular talent adds a necessary dimension to the group's ability to solve a problem and generate innovations.

Fostering cohesion entails having all members of the group involved with the contending forces at work in a project and being invested in the solution. The honesty, frankness, and directness in communications that are required to keep a project on track do not emerge from patronizing attitudes and behaviors. Decisive action, undertaken with ample understanding, serves everyone in the group by keeping the channels of communication clear and open.

4. *Concentration.* In an ideal sequence of events, a project would become focused over time, and the haggling over alternatives would quiet down as the group moved through the phases of development. But quite often the opposite happens: New ideas come up, and outside forces change direction and priorities and withdraw promised resources. All these factors diminish the ability of the working group to meet their internally motivated goals.

The manager of the co-involvement model has the difficult task of balancing the enthusiasm of the working group for new ideas and insights with meeting the requirements of a schedule, quality, and consistency. It also means balancing the larger organization's mission and resources with the demands of the working group. This means acting as a gatekeeper to outside influences and acting as a judge and jury inside the group. Much of the tension this system generates comes from this set of problems. Co-involvement requires the time and effort to enlist the group in arriving at a solution that preserves the program and/ or enriches it with the new input or else preserves it against encroachment.

5. *Conflation.* Finally, when these aspects of managerial effort come together, co-involvement attempts to multiply or leverage (to use the terminology of Andy Grove) the effect of the resources brought to bear on the project. The aim of managerial strategy is to recognize and capitalize on the company's wealth of human capital by combining resources in a well-thought-out manner that energizes all the parties involved.

THE STRATEGY MANAGEMENT MATRIX

At this point we have accumulated an imposing series of lists that purport to elucidate managerial issues in a value-based strategy. Let's take a moment to review them.

We have listed five managerial *functions*: customer consciousness, communications, control, consistency, and continuity. These are the intellectually oriented processes that keep the organization working together, on track and on time, as it fulfills its role of providing enablements.

Then, in this chapter we have listed *lower organizational roles and upper strategic roles* that managers often assume in the course of executing these functions. We have noted several *personality types* that are most successful in any organization but bring especially important qualities of attention and effort to value-based organization. And finally, we noted the particular *skills* people need in order to accomplish objectives in these kinds of organizations. If we put all these factors together, they add up to a new "demography," a new style of management than what we have been accustomed to under classical regimes.

To help us grasp the difference, I have devised a managerial matrix table (see Table 15.1) that shows how the managerial functions are executed in the form of roles, skills, and output in the context of classical and value-based strategies. I have also correlated Quinn's effective personality types to the kinds of functions they seem to perform best.

We can draw several conclusions from this matrix that help to summarize many of the points we have been developing throughout this volume.

First, the function that is believed to most account for profits is different in each strategic setting. For the capital strategist, profits will come from managerial consistency, from containing problems, and from maximizing the use of resources in place. For the classical manager, profits come from exercising control, leveraging resources to the maximum in the markets already established from products. For the value manager, customer consciousness and awareness of customer requirements constitute the key. The function of customer consciousness is of no consequence at all in the capital-based strategy.

Second, the classical systems rely on reports and written accounts of events, whereas a value strategy concentrates on creating the value flow in all its functions, maintaining its customer focus and organizational and production flexibility and adaptability.

Third, the value manager has to call on many more roles and skills than do the classical managers of either the capital or management type. The capital manager's role is director, pure and simple, and the skills most called on are the exercise of power and monitoring others' work. The classical manager's skills and roles are somewhat more diverse, but since they are obliged to meet the requirements of their capital strategist superiors, a great deal of their energies are concentrated in what Quinn has identified as the lower roles, roles that have little in the way of initiative and interpersonal sensitivity involved.

The manager who uses value strategy, however, is required to assume many diverse roles and must call on many different skills in order to accomplish the very creative and highly interpersonal and interactive objectives. A holographic organization that operates by maintaining a value flow through its production process is thus one that is very demanding and challenging for any manager.

So what this review shows is that to manage a value production strategy, or to institute co-involvement strategic management, is not a matter of one person's charisma or "leadership qualities." To the contrary, co-

Table 15.1

Strategy Management Matrix: Manager's Strategic Roles (R), Skills (S), and Output (O) as Reflected in Management Personality Types, Functions and in Three Types of Production Strategies

Management Function		Customer Consciousness / Conceptual Producers	Communications / Team Builders and Open Adaptives	Control / Aggressive Achievers	Consistency / Masters	Continuity and Innovation / Committed Intensives
Personality Strategy Type Suited to Function						
Capital-Based Strategy	R	——	Director	Director	Monitor	Director/Patriarch
	S	——	Order; Delegation	Measurement/Evaluation	Measurement	Power/Exemplar
	O	——	Memo	Zero Defects	Report/ROI	Policy
Management-Based Strategy	R	Monitor	Co-ordinator	Director	Producer	Director
	S	Survey/Analysis	Memo/Meeting	Power/Measurement	Efficiency/Routine	Report/Analysis
	O	Report/Market Share	Consensus	Optimize Resources ROI	Productivity	Policy
Value-Based Strategy	R	Innovator	Facilitator	Broker	Mentor	Mentor/Facilitator/Broker
	S	Commitment	Cohesion	Conflation	Concentration	Choice
	O	Value/Profit Discernment, Transactional Production	Discernment/Operational Production	Effectiveness	Quality	Discernment/Operational Production

involvement requires the ability to elicit the qualities out of a wide sector of the working group in such a way that the group's success is not dependent on any *one* person but is dependent on what *each* person brings to the table. It also means being able to assemble people into the kinds of groups where talents mix and blend; to assign "mentors" to younger workers, as do the Gores; and to put people who are more comfortable with ambiguity in positions to help and clarify goals and situations for people who are less comfortable in those situations.

It also means protecting and nurturing the talents of those whose abilities or personalities seem to be more limited than those of others. This calls for both a clear conception of what the project entails and a fierce defense of the project, over time, against encroachment, bureaucratic smothering, or inertia and complacency within the group.

CONCLUSION

In all honesty, we must, in the final analysis, say that this kind of organization is probably not for everyone. To people who are insecure about themselves, it might indeed be a threatening environment. To others who need structure and routine, this kind of environment might be too chaotic.

To owners who want their imprimatur on everything that comes out of their establishment, this kind of organization might leave them feeling abandoned and less than fulfilled. With a value-based strategy, the business's continuity and identity emanate not from the dictates of a top-down hierarchical structure but from the process that creates a group 'awareness and sensitivity to a viable value relationship.

An organization that is not able to work in this way may indeed have the resources and stature to survive and even thrive in the volatile world of turnover. But then again, as we have seen time and time again in the past decade, no matter how strong and mighty the organization is, no matter how deep its pockets, it just may not survive. Value strategy may not be a fast ticket to success either. But value-based co-involvement strategy has worked in the most volatile and difficult of industries to the success and enrichment of all involved—owners, shareholders, and customers. It has proved itself to be a strategy equal to the tasks and challenges posed by the new world of business.

NOTES

1. "Farewell, Fast Track," *Business Week*, December 10, 1990, pp. 196–197.
2. Robert E. Quinn, *Beyond Rational Management: Mastering the Paradoxes and Competing Demands of High Performance* (San Francisco: Jossey-Bass, 1988).

Glossary

attractor A core product or service within an enablement category. A product, such as an automobile, that occupies a place of prominence in people's hierarchy of enablements—in this case, the enablement category of personal transportation—and that gathers around it other supporting products that likewise become necessary or at least desirable. *See also* enablement category; position.

benefits The outcomes a buyer can expect from a product or service. Usually expressed in terms of *product* benefits, which derive directly from the product, or *company* benefits, which pertain to the special ways the business treats customers. We also cite *interactive* benefits, which constitute considerations of the experiences a buyer will have while using the product or engaging the service.

business A socially sanctioned organization that provides people with products and services they use to participate in activities in their daily lives, at work and at home.

capital A fund that provides a means of payment for a business to undertake new directions in carrying out its mission.

capital-based strategy A type of classical strategy, formulated by a capital strategist or exclusive group of planners, for others to follow more or less by rote, designed to direct a company's resources and energies toward increasing ROI.

classical strategy An explicit pattern or framework, devised by a central group of "planners," that is prescribed for others to follow in order to combine resources and actions in an attempt to gain competitive advantage, market share, profits, or ROI.

co-involvement A form of work relationship conceived under value production strategy in which all workers and managers involved in a program share in the formulation and implementation of strategies, innovations, and solutions. *See also* holographic organization.

competition The process a business engages so as to carefully define and meet customers' requirements for a satisfying quality experience with an activity and its enabling products and, in so doing, gain acceptance for that product or service (against other companies offering similar products) and establish a long-term value relationship.

culture The actual way a business conducts its external and internal relationships. The constituents of external relationships are means, measurement, and malleability; the constituents of how the organization maintains its internal relationships are words, walls, wages, and will.

deal The first kind of transaction that takes place during a valuing process. In this transaction, a price is set between a buyer and a business. The price reflects the outcome of a negotiation that sets the terms by which the buyer will judge the outcome of the subsequent enablement transaction. Steps of the deal are shopping, appraisal, negotiation, and exchange.

differentiation The process by means of which makers of related or similar products and services distinguish themselves in their markets. *See also* competition, integration.

discernment The first moment in the value flow of the production process (*see* value flow) in which attention is focused on customers' actual use of the product or service. Customers' interactions are monitored with the intent to develop opportunities for enhancement and innovation.

domain The suppliers and vendors, business and professional groups, distributors, associated producers, and even competitors that compose a viable enablement category (or industry, such as the automobile industry or the computer industry). An independent maker of windshields is part of the domain of an automaker; an independent software producer is part of a computer maker's domain.

enablement A term used in three ways in value strategy that are crucial to understanding this approach to decision making. First, enablement names a kind of *transaction* that takes place during a valuing process. The enablement transaction is the cornerstone of the value relationship in that it encompasses all expectations, actions, experiences, and judgments a person has about the product or service in question. The transaction encompasses all the ways people interact with their world in a way that is only possible— achieves outcomes that are only possible—by means of this kind of product or service. Second, *enablement* is used to distinguish the *valued* component of a product from the actual product or service that is consumed, used up, or worn out during the course of its use. The commodity is valued because the product or service makes an activity possible and/or desirable; that is, it enables a person to participate in this activity. Thus, while the idea of enablement is based on the experience with a single product, more important, it considers all similar products to be equal or comparable insofar as they enable people to take part in the same activity. The buyer's ability to engage the world in a chosen way is the focus, not the single product that had been purchased this time. Finally, an enabling product is distinct from a product that satisfies a need in that an enabling product involves choice about which product to use, and it is applied to those areas of life over which people want to exercise some control. A need cannot be chosen and its means of satisfaction are not controlled.

enablement category Different enabling products that function together as a group and make it possible for people to carry out life-style activities in an acceptable manner. Automobile insurance protects people's (and financing companies') investment in an automobile and is part of that category that is centered by the automobile. *See also* attractor; micromarkets; position.

holographic organization The kind of organization in which each member carries forward information about the whole in all decisions. As in a hologram, if members of the organization are broken off (not included in the organization's growth and development), the image loses clarity and becomes blurred and thus less effective. *See also* co-involvement.

increasing returns A macroeconomic theory that states that when a product comes to dominate an industry, market, or enablement category, it gathers around it an increasing number of supporting elements, such as complementary technologies or wide distribution. When the product takes on the mantle of being a "standard" or core product, it, in turn, creates the "snowball" effect of generating more product opportunities and increasing sales. Since it envisions such growth in opportunities for product and service offerings as well as for increased sales, as acceptance grows and expands in influence, the theory of increasing returns runs counter to the idea that as markets mature, they offer producers only increased competition and thus decreasing returns. *See also* turnover.

integration The process by means of which businesses ensure that all the necessary provisions for the use, selling, and servicing of their products and services are in place and available to customers and potential buyers. It is one of the three actions that businesses engage in so as to create their market or establish themselves as or within an enablement category, the others being differentiation and competition. *See also* competition; differentiation; enablement category; markets.

labor (as capital) Labor conceived as a fund of experience that can be applied when a business has to undertake changes in its products and/or organization. This fund of experience provides the intelligence and will necessary to make turnover-induced changes successfully and cost-effectively. *See also* capital; social capital.

management The oversight and assessing processes, operating procedures, and decision making that go into making and maintaining an organization. Management includes instilling customer consciousness into the business, maintaining and fostering communications, exerting cost and productivity controls, maintaining consistency of quality and effort, and maintaining the organization's continuity over time as it decides what to change and what to preserve. We make the distinction between these management "functions"—in which everyone in an organization can participate and for which everyone can assume some appropriate level of responsibility—and management "positions"—which are parceled out sparingly in an ever narrowing hierarchical manner.

management-based strategy A type of classical strategy that uses various tactics such as cost leadership, differentiating product features, and/or market focus in order to gain and maintain market share as a means to increase return on investment.

markets Real or conceived arenas of action wherein different producers establish similar products and services and then compete for the attention and loyalty of customers, which can lead to profit-making value relationships. Owing to factors such as advancing technology, social change, and international competition, markets are subject to volatile upheavals (*see* turnover) and ever growing specialization (*see* competition; enablement category; micromarkets).

market style The constitution of a market, industry, or enablement category at a particular point in time, which has distinctive characteristics determined by the configuration of leading products, technologies, and distribution methods, among other factors.

micromarkets Small, highly specialized groupings of customers, each of which requires close tailoring of products and services to their requirements.

mission An expression of a business's essential relationship to its customers, first and foremost, as well as other stakeholders, including employees, shareholders, and the community in which the business resides or the communities its products and/or services serve.

need A basic and fundamental biological, physiological, or psychological impulse or compulsion to resolve a lack or deficiency of the body or in the environment. A need arises repetitiously and is satisfied by the most efficient means available, with little or no choice or forethought. *See also* enablement.

operational production The second moment in the value flow (*see* value flow) of the production process in which members of an organization pay attention to the ways they work together in order to make decisions about how operations will progress from an idea's conception through its sale and acceptance by customers. *See also* co-involvement; discernment; production; transactional production.

organizational strategy A strategy designed to keep an organization flexible and responsible in the face of changing customer demand and market turbulence. A value organization strategy seeks to create a holographic organization. *See also* holographic organization; turnover.

position The potential for profitability as a function of a product's or service's position within buyers' hierarchies of enablements and/or proximity to (or level of integration with) a core product or service within an enablement category. *See also* increasing returns; profit.

procurement The final stage in the experiential aspect of the valuing process when people appropriate products or services, incorporate them into their lives, use them, and finally reconsider or evaluate the products in advance of a decision as to whether or not to repurchase them. *See also* projection; prospection; value process.

production The process of ensuring that all necessary resources, energies, and talents are organized effectively so as to meet the requirements of a business's value relationship. *See also* value relationship.

profit A necessary outcome from a business's efforts to meet customer requirements if it is to continue in existence. In value strategy, profit derives from a product's or service's "position" (*see* position) in a particular enablement category vis-à-vis an attractor or core enablement (*see* attractor).

projection The second stage in the experiential aspect of the valuing process, when people consciously consider how prospective purchases of products and/or services will fit into the actual course of their daily lives. They eliminate some options based on criteria of whether or not some choices actually fit with their current conditions and circumstances. *See also* procurement; prospection; value process.

prospection The first stage in the experiential aspect of the valuing process, when people commit to action in order to resolve a desire or lack in their situations by means of known or envisioned products or services made available by businesses. *See also* procurement; projection; value process.

quality The essential characteristics of a product or service that come to the fore of customers' attention in the course of meeting their requirements. Quality encompasses both the experience and the evaluation of that experience during the time customers participated in activities by using the product or service.

social capital A fund of resources provided by public tax revenues that enable businesses to undertake production and changes in production. Roads, for example, facilitate transportation and distribution; the public education system provides a work force suited for the needs of production. *See also* capital; labor (as capital).

strategy The process by means of which business decision makers contend with and generate change in products and services as well as their own organizations and production processes.

transactional production The final moment of the value flow in the production process. In this moment, members of the organization pay attention to how people interact with the product once it is in their hands—when people are using the product or service and are evaluating whether or not they will repurchase the product when the time comes. *See also* benefits; discernment; operational production.

turnover A phenomenon of market change that denotes the obsolescence of products and even whole industries or enablement categories, brought about at increasingly rapid intervals owing to the competitive pressures brought on by changes in technologies, social conditions, new product ideas, and so on.

value The relative worth of products or services as determined by a complex process that incorporates an individual's experience (*see* procurement; projection; prospection) and transactions between people (*see* deal) and between people and the products and services they purchase (*see* enablement). The value of a product or service is expressed in price, which is determined by competition with similar or comparable goods in markets. When making their determinations, buyers in the market not only consider the specific product or service at hand but also factor in a host of surrounding and supportive products that connect with other aspects of life and life activities in the form of an enablement category. *See also* enablement; enablement category; markets; value process.

value flow A qualitative means of evaluating the production process that assesses how each position and each operation contributes to making the business's value relationship a success. *See also* discernment; operational production; transactional production.

value process The experiential and transactional steps involved in determining the value of a product or service. *See also* deal; enablement; procurement; projection; prospection; value.

value relationship A reciprocal, long-term relationship between a business and its customers that arises when a business provides, supports, and enhances products and services that enable buyers to engage in certain activities in their daily lives, at work and at home. A value relationship is established when both the business and its customers, respectively, count on each other to engage in the activity supported by the product and the activities required to produce it.

value strategy The concepts, decisions, and actions that are necessary to establish, sustain, and enhance a more or less necessary relationship between a business and customers. *See also* value relationship.

Bibliography

Adizes, Ichak. *Corporate Lifecycles: How and Why Corporations Grow and Die and What to Do About It.* Englewood Cliffs, N.J.: Prentice-Hall, 1988.

Anderson, Paul F. "Marketing, Strategic Planning and the Theory of the Firm." In *Marketing Theory: Distinguished Contributors,* Stephen W. Brown and Raymond P. Fisk, eds. New York: John Wiley, 1984.

Andrall, E. Pearson. "Six Basics for General Managers." *Harvard Business Review,* July–August 1989, pp. 94–101.

Andrews, Kenneth R. *The Concept of Corporate Strategy.* Homewood, Ill.: Richard D. Irwin, 1980.

Anshen, Melvin. "The Management of Ideas." In *Strategic Management, Harvard Business Review Executive Book Series,* Richard G. Hamermesh, ed. New York: John Wiley, 1983.

Ansoff, H. Igor. *The New Corporate Strategy.* New York: John Wiley, 1988.

———. *Strategic Management.* London: Macmillan, 1979.

Appadurai, Argun. *The Social Life of Things: Commodities in Cultural Perspective.* New York: Cambridge University Press, 1986.

Arendt, Hannah. *The Human Condition.* Chicago: University of Chicago Press, 1958.

Argyris, Chris. *Integrating the Individual and the Organization.* New York: John Wiley, 1964.

———. *Organization and Innovation.* Homewood, Ill.: Richard D. Irwin, 1965.

Argyris, Chris, and Donald A. Schon, *Organizational Learning.* Reading, Mass.: Addison-Wesley, 1978.

Arthur, W. Brian. "Competing Technologies and Economic Prediction." *Options,* April 1984, pp. 10–13.

———. "Competing Technologies, Increasing Returns, and Lock-In by Historical Events." *Economic Journal* 99 (March 1989): 116–131.

———. "Positive Feedbacks in the Economy." *Scientific American*, February 1990, pp. 92–95.

———. "Self-Reinforcing Mechanisms in Economics." In *The Economy as an Evolving Complex System*, P. W. Anderson, K. J. Arrow, and D. Pines, eds. Reading, Mass.: Addison-Wesley, 1988.

Baatz, Elizabeth B. "The Changing Face of the Organization," *Electronic Business*, March 18, 1991.

Bagozzi, Richard P. "Marketing as Exchange." In *Marketing Theory: Distinguished Contributors*, Stephen W. Brown and Raymond P. Fisk, eds. New York: Wiley, 1984.

Beckhard, Richard, and Reuben T. Harris. *Organizational Transitions: Managing Complex Change*. Reading, Mass.: Addison-Wesley, 1977.

Bellah, Robert N., Richard Madsen, William M. Sullivan, Ann Swidler, and Steven Tipton. *Habits of the Heart: Individualism and Commitment in American Life*. New York: Harper & Row, 1985.

Below, Patrick J., George L. Morrisey, and Betty L. Acomb. *The Executive Guide to Strategic Planning*. San Francisco: Jossey-Bass, 1987.

Benton, Raymond, Jr. "Work, Consumption and the Joyless Consumer." In *Philosophical and Radical Thought in Marketing*, A. Fuat Firat, Nikhilesh Dholakia, and Richard P. Bagozzi, eds. Lexington, Mass.: D. C. Heath, 1987.

Bluestone, Barry, and Bennett Harrison. *The Deindustrialization of America*. New York: Basic Books, 1982.

Bohm-Bawerk, Eugene. *Capital and Interest. Positive Theory of Capital*, vol. 2, George D. Huncke, trans. South Holland, Ill.: Libertarian Press, 1959.

Braudel, Fernand. *Capitalism and Material Life, 1400–1800*. New York: Harper & Row, 1973.

Burgelman, Robert A. "Corporate Entrepreneurship and Strategic Management: Insights from a Process Study." *Management Science* 29, no. 12, December 1983: 1349–1364.

Burrough, Bryan, and John Helyar. *Barbarians at the Gate: The Fall of RJR Nabisco*. New York: Harper & Row, 1990.

Campbell, Andrew, and Kiran Tawadey. *Mission and Business Philosophy: Winning Employee Commitment*. Oxford, England: Heinemann, 1990.

Chandler, Alfred D., Jr. *Strategy and Structure*. Cambridge, Mass.: MIT Press, 1962.

———. *The Visible Hand: The Managerial Revolution in American Business*. Cambridge, Mass.: Belknap Press, 1977.

Chernow, Ron. *The House of Morgan: An American Banking Dynasty and the Rise of Modern Finance*. New York: Atlantic Monthly Press, 1990.

Collier, P., and D. Horowitz. *The Fords: An American Epic*. New York: Summit Books, 1987.

Crosby, Lawrence A., and Darrel D. Muehling. "External Variables on the Fishbein Model: Mediation, Moderation or Direct Effects?" *Advances in Consumer Research* 10 (1982): 94–98.

Csikszentmihalyi, Mihaly. *Flow: The Psychology of Optimal Experience*. New York: Harper & Row, 1990.

Csikszentmihalyi, Mihaly, and E. Rochberg-Halton. *The Meaning of Things: Domestic Symbols and the Self*. New York: Cambridge University Press, 1981.

Davidow, W. H., and Bro Utal. "Service Companies, Focus or Falter." *Harvard Business Review*, July–August 1989, pp. 77–85.

Davidson, Andrew R., and Diane M. Morrison. "Social Psychological Models of Decision Making." In *Choice Models for Buyer Behavior*, McAlister Leigh, ed. Greenwich, Conn.: JAI Press, 1982.

Day, Ellen, and Stephen B. Castleberry. "Defining and Evaluating Quality: The Consumer's View." *Advances in Consumer Research* 13 (1985): 94–98.

Dewey, John. "The Field of 'Value.'" In *Value, A Cooperative Inquiry*, Ray Lepley, ed. New York: Columbia University Press, 1949.

———. "Some Questions About Value." In *Value, A Cooperative Inquiry*, Ray Lepley, ed. New York: Columbia University Press, 1949.

———. "Theory of Valuation." In *Foundations of the Unity of Science*, vol. 2, Otto Neurath, Rudolf Carnap, and Charles Morris, eds. Chicago: University of Chicago Press, 1970.

Dholakia, Nikhilesh, A. Fuat Firat, and Richard P. Bagozzi. "Rethinking Marketing." In *Philosophical and Radical Thought in Marketing*, Firat, Dholakia, and Bagozzi, eds. Lexington, Mass.: D. C. Heath, 1987.

Dobb, Maurice. *Studies in the Development of Capitalism*. New York: International Publishers, 1947.

———. *Innovation and Entrepreneurship*. New York: Harper & Row, 1985.

———. *Management: Tasks, Responsibilities, Practices*. New York: Harper & Row, 1974.

———. *Managing for Results*. New York: Harper & Row, 1964.

———. *Managing in Turbulent Times*. New York: Harper & Row, 1980.

Eells, Richard, and Clarence Walton. *Conceptual Foundations of Business*. Homewood, Ill.: Richard D. Irwin, 1961.

Firat, A. Fuat. "The Social Construction of Consumption Patterns: Understanding Macro Consumption Patterns." In *Philosophical and Radical Thought in Marketing*, A. Fuat Firat, Nikhilesh Dholakia, and Richard P. Bagozzi, eds. Lexington, Mass.: D. C. Heath, 1987.

Fishbein, M., and I. Ajzen. "Attitude and the Prediction of Behavior." In *Readings in Attitude Theory and Measurement*, Martin Fishbein, ed. New York: John Wiley, 1967.

———. *Belief, Attitude, Intention and Behavior*. Reading, Mass.: Addison-Wesley, 1975.

———. "An Investigation of the Relationship Between Beliefs About an Object and the Attitude Toward that Object." *Human Relations* 16 (1963): 233–240.

———. *Understanding Attitudes and Predicting Social Behavior*. Englewood Cliffs, N.J.: Prentice-Hall, 1980.

Foucault, Michel. *The Order of Things: An Archaeology of the Human Sciences*. New York: Random House, 1973.

Freeman, R. Edward. *Strategic Management, A Stakeholder Approach*. Boston: Pitman, 1984.

Fullerton, Ronald A. "The Poverty of Historical Analysis: Present Weakness and Future Cure in U.S. Marketing Thought." In *Philosophical and Radical Thought in Marketing*, A. Fuat Firat, Nikhilesh Dholakia, and Richard P. Bagozzi, eds. Lexington, Mass.: D. C. Heath, 1987.

Furse, David H., Garish N. Punj, and David W. Stewart. "Individual Search Strategies in New Automobile Purchases." *Advances in Consumer Research* 9 (1981): 379–384.

Galbraith, John K. *The Affluent Society*. Boston: Houghton Mifflin, 1958.

Geneen, Harold. *Managing*. New York: Doubleday, 1984.

Gilbert, Daniel R., Jr., Edwin Hartman, John J. Mauriel, and R. Edward Freeman. *A Logic for Strategy*. Cambridge, Mass.: Ballinger, 1988.

Gleick, James. *Chaos: Making a New Science*. New York: Penguin Books, 1987.

Granzin, Kent L. "A Proposed Path Toward Marketing Theory . . . By Means of the Value Relation." In *Marketing Theory: Philosophy of Science Perspectives*, Ronald F. Bush and Shelby D. Hunt, eds. Chicago: American Marketing Association, 1982.

Greider, William. *Secrets of the Temple: How the Federal Reserve Runs the Country*. New York: Simon and Schuster, 1987.

Gronhaug, Kjill, and Nikhilesh Dholakia. "Consumers, Markets and Supply Systems: A Perspective on Marketization and Its Effects." In *Philosophical and Radical Thought in Marketing*, A. Fuat Firat, Nikhilesh Dholakia, and Richard P. Bagozzi, eds. Lexington, Mass.: D. C. Heath, 1987.

Grove, Andrew S. *High Output Management*. New York: Random House, 1983.

Halberstam, David. *The Reckoning*. New York: Avon Books, 1986.

Hassard, John, and Sudi Sharifi. "Corporate Culture and Strategic Change." *Journal of General Management* 15, no. 2 (Winter 1989): 4–19.

Hayes, Robert H. "Why Japanese Factories Work." *Harvard Business Review*, July–August 1981, pp. 56–66.

Hayes, Robert H., and William J. Abernathy. "Managing Our Way to Economic Decline." In *Strategic Management, Harvard Business Review Executive Book Series*, Richard G. Hamermesh, ed. New York: John Wiley, 1983.

Hayes, Robert H., and Kim B. Clark. "Why Some Factories Are More Productive Than Others." *Harvard Business Review*, September–October, 1986, pp. 66–73.

Hayes, Robert H., and Ramchandran Jaikuman. "Manufacturing Crisis: New Technologies, Obsolete Organizations." *Harvard Business Review*, September–October 1988, pp. 77–85.

Hegel, G.W.F. *Phenomenology of Spirit*, A. V. Miller, trans. New York: Oxford University Press, 1977.

———. *The Philosophy of History*, J. Sibree, trans. New York: Dover, 1956.

———. *The Philosophy of Right*, T. M. Knox, trans. New York: Oxford University Press, 1967.

———. *The Science of Logic*, A. V. Miller, trans. Atlantic Highlands, N.J.: Humanities Press International, 1989.

Hendry, John. "Barriers to Excellence and the Politics of Innovation." *Journal of General Management* 15, no. 2 (Winter 1989): 20–31.

Herzberg, Frederick. "One More Time: How Do You Motivate Employees?" In *The Great Writings in Management and Organizational Behavior*, Louis E.

Boone and Donald D. Bowen, ed. Tulsa, Okla.: Petroleum Publishing, 1980.

Holbrook, Morris B. "O, Consumer, How You've Changed: Some Radical Reflections on the Roots of Consumption." In *Philosophical and Radical Thought in Marketing*, A. Fuat Firat, Nikhilesh Dholakia, and Richard P. Bagozzi, eds. Lexington, Mass.: D. C. Heath, 1987.

Holland, Max. *When the Machine Stopped: A Cautionary Tale from American Industry.* Boston: Harvard Business School Press, 1989.

Horsky, Don, and Subrata K. Sen. "Models of Choice: Perspectives from Psychology, Social Psychology, Economics and Marketing." In *Choice Models for Buyer Behavior*, McAlister Leigh, ed. Greenwich, Conn.: JAI Press, 1982.

House, Robert J., and Terrence R. Mitchell. "Path-Goal Theory of Leadership." In *The Great Writings in Management and Organizational Behavior*, Louis E. Boone, and Donald D. Bowen, eds. Tulsa, Okla.: Petroleum Publishing, 1980.

Hoyer, Wayne D. "Variations in Choice Strategies Across Decisions Contexts: An Examination of Contingent Factors." *Advances in Consumer Research* 13 (1985): 32–36.

Hunt, E. K., and Jesse G. Schwartz, eds. *A Critique of Economic Theory.* Baltimore, Md.: Penguin, 1972.

Husserl, Edmund. *Cartesian Meditations: An Introduction to Phenomenology*, Dorion Cairns, trans. The Hague: Martinus Hijhoff, 1969.

———. *The Idea of Phenomenology*, W. P. Alston and G. Nakhnikian, trans. The Hague: Martinus Nijhoff, 1964.

———. *Ideas: General Introduction to Pure Phenomenology*, W. R. Boyce Gibson, trans. London: Collier, 1962.

Iacocca, Lee. *Iacocca: An Autobiography.* New York: Bantam, 1984.

Jaikuman, Ramchandran. "Post Industrial Manufacturing." *Harvard Business Review*, November–December 1986, pp. 70–78.

Kahle, L. R., and P. Kennedy. "Using the List of Values (LOV) to Understand Consumers." *Journal of Consumer Marketing* 6, no. 3 (Summer 1989): 5–12.

Kanter, Rosabeth Moss. *The Change Masters: Innovation and Entrepreneurship in the American Corporation.* New York: Simon & Schuster, 1983.

———. "When a Thousand Flowers Bloom: Structural, Collective and Social Conditions for Innovation in Organization." In *Research in Organizational Behavior*, vol. 10, Barry M. Staw and L. L. Cummings, eds. Greenwich, Conn.: JAI Press, 1988.

———. *When Giants Learn to Dance.* New York: Simon & Schuster, 1989.

Karasek, Robert, and Tores Theorelli. *Healthy Work: Stress, Productivity and the Reconstruction of Working Life.* New York: Basic Books, 1990.

Kidder, Tracy. *The Soul of a New Machine.* Boston: Atlantic—Little, Brown, 1981.

Kilbourne, William E. "Self-Actualization and the Consumption Process: Can You Get There from Here?" *Philosophical and Radical Thought in Marketing*, A. Fuat Firat, Nikhilesh Dholakia, and Richard P. Bagozzi, eds. Lexington, Mass.: D. C. Heath, 1987.

Kohut, Heinz. *The Restoration of the Self.* New York: International University Press, 1977.

Kotler, Philip. "A Generic Concept of Marketing." In *Marketing Theory: Distinguished Contributors,* Stephen W. Brown and Raymond P. Fisk, eds. New York: John Wiley, 1984.

———. "Humanistic Marketing: Beyond the Marketing Concept." In *Philosophical and Radical Thought in Marketing,* A. Fuat Firat, Nikhilesh Dholakia, and Richard P. Bagozzi, eds. Lexington, Mass.: D. C. Heath, 1987.

LaFeif, William C., and O'Neal. "Process of Developing Commitment in the Industrial Buyer-Seller Relationship." *American Marketing Association Proceedings (Marketing Theory)* (1987): 121–124.

Lawler, Edward E., III, and Lyman W. Porter. "The Effects of Performance on Job Satisfaction." *Industrial Relations* 7, no. 1 (October 1967): 20–28.

Levitt, Theodore. *The Marketing Imagination.* New York: Free Press, 1986.

———. "Marketing Intangible Products and Product Intangibles." *Harvard Business Review,* May–June 1981, pp. 94–102.

McGregor, Douglas. *The Human Side of Enterprise.* New York: McGraw-Hill, 1960.

Mahatoo, Winston. "A Case for Differentiating Motives from Needs, Drives, Wants." *American Marketing Association Proceedings (Marketing Theory)* (1987): 217–220.

Mandel, Ernest. *Marxist Economic Theory,* vols. 1 and 2, Brian Pearce, trans. New York: Monthly Review Press, 1970.

Marcuse, Herbert. *Eros and Civilization: A Philosophical Inquiry into Freud.* New York: Random House, 1962.

———. *One Dimensional Man.* Boston: Beacon Press, 1966.

Marx, Karl. *Capital,* vols. 1–3, Frederick Engels, ed. Samuel Moore and Edward Aveling, trans. New York: International Publishers, 1967.

———. *Contribution to the Critique of Political Economy.* Moscow: Progress Publishers, 1970.

———. *The Economic and Philosophic Manuscripts of 1844,* M. Milligan, trans. New York: International Publishers, 1964.

———. *Theories of Surplus Value,* vols. 1–3. Moscow: Progress Publishers, 1969.

Maslow, Abraham H. *Motivation and Personality.* New York: Harper & Row, 1970.

Miles, R. E., and C. C. Snow. "Organizations: New Concepts for New Forms." *California Business Review* 28, no. 3 (Spring 1986): 66–73.

Mills, D. Quinn. *Rebirth of the Corporation.* New York: John Wiley, 1991.

Mintzberg, Henry. "The Design School: Reconsidering the Basic Premises of Strategic Management." *Strategic Management Journal* 11 (1990): 171–195.

———. *Structures in Fives: Designing Effective Organizations.* Englewood Cliffs, N.J.: Prentice-Hall, 1983.

Mooriman, Christine. "Marketing as Technique: The Influence of Marketing on the Meanings of Consumption." In *Philosophical and Radical Thought in Marketing,* A. Fuat Firat, Nikhilesh Dholakia, and Richard P. Bagozzi, eds. Lexington, Mass.: D. C. Heath, 1987.

Morgan, Gareth. *Images of Organization.* Newbury Park, Calif.: Sage, 1986.

———. *Riding the Waves of Change: Developing Managerial Competence for a Turbulent World.* San Francisco: Jossey-Bass, 1989.

Morgan, Gareth, ed. *Beyond Method: Strategies for Social Research*. Beverly Hills, Calif.: Sage, 1983.

Morgan, Gareth, and Linda Smircich. "The Case for Qualitative Research." In *Marketing Theory: Distinguished Contributors*, Stephen W. Brown and Raymond P. Fisk, eds. New York: John Wiley, 1984.

Nicosia, Francesco M. *Consumer Decision Processes, Marketing and Advertising Implications*. Englewood Cliffs, N.J.: Prentice-Hall, 1966.

Nishida, Kitaro. *Art and Morality*, David A. Dilworth and Valdo H. Viglielmo, trans. Honolulu: University of Hawaii Press, 1973.

———. *Fundamental Problems of Philosophy*, David A. Dilworth, trans. Tokyo: Sophia University, 1970.

———. *An Inquiry into the Good*, Masao Abe and Christopher Lee, trans. New Haven, Conn.: Yale University Press, 1990.

———. *Intuition and Reflection in Self-Consciousness*, Valdo H. Viglielmo, trans. Albany: State University of New York Press, 1987.

———. *Nothingness and the Religious Worldview*, David A. Dilworth, trans. Honolulu: University of Hawaii Press, 1987.

Nozick, Robert. *The Examined Life*. New York: Simon & Schuster, 1989.

Ouchi, William G. *Theory Z: How American Business Can Meet the Japanese Challenge*. Reading, Mass.: Addison-Wesley, 1981.

Ouchi, William G., and Jerry G. Johnson. "Types of Organizational Control and Their Relationship to Emotional Well-Being." *Administrative Science Quarterly* 23 (June 1978): 293–317.

Pascale, Richard T., and Anthony G. Athos. *The Art of Japanese Management*. New York: Simon & Schuster, 1981.

Patterson, James, and Peter Kim. *The Day America Told the Truth: What People Really Believe About Everything That Really Matters*. Englewood Cliffs, N.J.: Prentice-Hall, 1991.

Penrose, Roger. *The Emperor's New Mind: Concerning Computers, Minds and the Laws of Physics*. New York: Oxford University Press, 1989.

Pepper, Stephen C. "Observations on Value from an Analysis of a Simple Appetition." In *Value, a Cooperative Inquiry*, Ray Lepley, ed. New York: Columbia University Press, 1949.

———. *The Sources of Value*. Berkeley: University of California Press, 1970.

Peters, Thomas J. "The Rational Model Has Led Us Astray." *Planning Review*, March 1982, pp. 16–23.

———. *Thriving in Chaos: Handbook for a Management Revolution*. New York: Knopf, 1987.

Peters, Thomas J., and Nancy Austin. *A Passion for Excellence: The Leadership Difference*. New York: Random House, 1985.

Peters, Thomas J., and Robert H. Waterman. *In Search of Excellence: Lessons from America's Best Run Companies*. New York: Harper & Row, 1982.

Polanyi, Karl. *The Great Transformation*. Boston: Beacon Press, 1957.

Porter, Michael E. *Competitive Strategy: Techniques for Analyzing Industries and Competitors*. New York: Free Press, 1980.

———. "How Competitive Forces Shape Strategy." In *Strategic Management, Harvard Business Review Executive Book Series*, Richard Hamermesh, ed. New York: John Wiley, 1983.

Quinn, James Brian. *Strategies for Change: Logical Incrementalism.* Homewood, Ill.: Richard D. Irwin, 1980.

Quinn, Robert E. *Beyond Rational Management: Mastering the Paradoxes and Competing Demands of High Performance.* San Francisco: Jossey-Bass, 1988.

Rayner, Bruce C. P., "A Blueprint for Competition." *Electronic Business,* March 18, 1991.

Robinson, Joan. *Economic Philosophy.* Chicago: Aldine, 1962.

Rubin, I. I. *Essays on Marx's Theory of Value.* Detroit: Black and Red, 1972.

Russell, Robert D. "How Organizational Culture Can Help to Institutionalize the Spirit of Innovation in Entrepreneurial Ventures." *Journal of Organizational Change Management* 2, no. 3 (1989): 7–15.

Sartre, Jean-Paul. *Search for a Method,* H. E. Barnes, trans. New York: Alfred A. Knopf, 1963.

Schein, Edgar H. *Organizational Culture and Leadership.* San Francisco: Jossey-Bass, 1985.

———. "Organizational Socialization and the Profession of Management." In *The Great Writings in Management and Organizational Behavior,* Louis E. Boone and Donald D. Bowen, ed. Tulsa, Okla.: Petroleum Publishing, 1980.

———. *Process Consultation: Its Role in Organization Development.* Reading, Mass.: Addison-Wesley, 1969.

Schumpeter, Joseph A. *Theory of Economic Development.* Cambridge, Mass.: Harvard University Press, 1934.

Seashore, Stanley E. "Criteria of Organizational Effectiveness." In *The Great Writings in Management and Organizational Behavior,* Louis E. Boone and Donald D. Bowen, eds. Tulsa, Okla.: Petroleum Publishing, 1980.

Senge, Peter M. *The Fifth Discipline: The Art and Practice of the Learning Organization.* New York: Doubleday/Currency, 1990.

Sheth, Jagdish N. "Consumer Behavior: Surpluses and Shortages." *Advances in Consumer Research* 9 (1981): 13–16.

Sheth, Jagdish N., and W. Wayne Talzrzyk. "Perceived Instrumentality and Value Importance as Determinants of Attitudes." *Journal of Market Research* 9 (February 1972).

Shrivastava, P., and S. A. Nadman. "Strategic Leadership Patterns." *Strategic Management Journal* 10 [Special] (Summer 1989).

Simmonds, Kenneth. "Marketing as Innovation, the Eighth Paradigm." *Journal of Management Studies* 23, no. 5 (September 1986): 479–500.

Sloan, Alfred P. *My Years with General Motors.* Garden City, N.Y.: Doubleday, 1963.

Snell, Bradford C. "American Ground Transport: A Proposal for Restructuring the Automotive, Truck, Bus and Rail Industries." Testimony to the Subcommittee on Antitrust and Monopoly of the Committee on the Judiciary of the U.S. Senate, February 26, 1974, pp. 28–32.

Takeuchi, Hirotaka, and Ikjiro Nonaka. "The New Product Development Game." *Harvard Business Review,* January–February 1986, pp. 137–146.

Thompson, C. J., W. B. Locander, and H. R. Pollio. "Putting Consumer Experience Back into Consumer Research: The Philosophy and Method of

Existential Phenomenology." *Journal of Consumer Research* 16, no. 2 (September 1989): 133–146.

Triandis, Harry C. "A Model of Choice in Marketing." In *Choice Models for Buyer Behavior*, McAlister Leigh, ed. Greenwich, Conn.: JAI Press, 1982.

Tversky, Amos, and Shmuel Sattath. "Preference Trees." In *Choice Models for Buyer Behavior*, McAlister Leigh, ed. Greenwich, Conn.: JAI Press, 1982.

Van de Ven, Andrew H. "Central Problems in the Management of Innovation." *Management Science* 32, no. 5 (May 1986): 590–607.

Vroom, Victor H. "A New Look at Managerial Decision Making." In *Great Writings in Management and Organizational Behavior*, Louis E. Boone and Donald D. Bowen, eds. Tulsa, Okla.: Petroleum Publishing, 1980.

Westley, F., and H. Mintzberg. "Visionary Leadership and Strategic Management." *Strategic Management Journal* 10 [Special] (Summer 1989): 17–32.

Wheelwright, Steven C. "Japan—Where Operations Really Are Strategic." *Harvard Business Review*, July–August 1981, pp. 67–74.

Young, Jeffrey S. *Steve Jobs: The Journey Is the Reward*. New York: Lynx Books, 1988.

Zaleznik, Abraham. "Managers and Leaders, Are They Different?" In *Strategic Management, Harvard Business Review Executive Book Series*, Richard G. Hamermesh, ed. New York: John Wiley, 1983.

Index

About the Author

MICHAEL H. SHENKMAN is a Senior Consultant at Mage Centers for Management Development. With more than twenty years experience in business, he has been an independent consultant for the past twelve years.